# Nebraska Farm Life WWI to WWII

To settle the A. C. McCall Estate will sell the following at public auction at the farm 2 miles South of Red Cloud, Nebraska, to the River Bridge, then 5 miles West on the River Road, or 3 miles East of the Inavale River Bridge on the River Road, on

# SATURDAY, NOVEMBER 18, *1972*

STARTING AT 11:00 a.m. SHARP.                         LINE PRECINCT CLUB WILL SERVE LUNCH.

## MACHINERY

John Deere 60 tractor, power-trol, Rol-o-Matic, good tires, good condition.
Massey Ferguson 35 tractor, good tires, good condition.
2-row 3-point Mounted weeder.
Ferguson 3-point mounted lister.
2-14 Three point plow.
Ford mounted hay buck with push-off.
Ford 3-point mounted scoop.
IHC 330 wheel type tandem disc.
John Deere No. 5 7-ft. power mower.
John Deere mounted lister.
John Deere 2-row picker.
McCormick No. 7 mower.
John Deere 2-row mounted cultivator.
John Deere 2-row weeder.
Farmhand F-10 hydraulic stacker with hay basket.
John Deere hammermill grinder.
Farmhand 6-wheel side delivery rake.
15-ft. Field packer.
John Deere 6-ft. oneway on steel.
IHC 3-16 plow on rubber.
Two 4-wheel rubber tired trailers with boxes.
26-ft. Elevator.
McCormick 8-16 grain drill on steel.
Wagon hoist.
IHC 2-row weeder.
10-ft. Dump hay rake.
Old grain binder.
2-Wheel flat bed trailer.
Two old hayracks on steel.
Three steel wheel wagons with boxes.
Case threshing machine.
2-Wheel trailer with stock racks.
Mounted posthole digger.
Corn planter.
10-ft. Field disc.    Drag.
2-Row horse drawn cultivator.
4-Section drag harrow.
300-gal. Fuel tank on steel stand.

## Antiques - Collectables
## Household Goods

Wicker rocker.    Leather seat rocker.
Square oak dining table.
Round oak dining table.
4 Oak dining chairs.
Old wooden rocker.
Old kerosene lamps.    Antique dresser.
5 Drawer oak chest.    Hall tree.
Oak dresser with mirror.
Wooden bed.    Old wall telephone.
Flat top trunk.    Old toys.
Iron kettle.    Oak arm rocker.
Some old harness.    Stadium seats.
Home brew equipment.
Old wood or coal heater.
Other antique items.    Cabinet base.
Electric console sewing machine.
Firestone electric range.
Maytag conventional washer.
4 Metal beds complete.    Misc. dishes.
Round card table.    4 Folding chairs.
Recliner chair.    Two hassocks.
Beige platform rocker.    Table lamp.
Two electric fans.    Record cabinet.
Beige studio couch.    Step ladder.
Porch swing.    Bookcase headboard.
8 Drawer chest drawers.
4 Drawer chest drawers.
Some bedding and towels.
Many other articles too numerous to mention.

### PICKUP

1972 Dodge ½-ton pickup, 4 wheel drive, 1,200 miles, like new.

## Tools and Miscellaneous

Mustang 7 riding mower.
Power lawn mower.    Tree trimmer.
50 Blocks cattle salt.    Forge.
Wards 225 amp. electric welder.
Air compressor.    Welding table.
Large anvil.    Large bench vise.
Bolt cutter.    Pipe dog.
Cob fork.    Chain saw.
Table saw.    Pipe wrenches.
Power Vac shop vacuum.
Battery charger.    Trouble light.
All kinds hand tools.
Electric power saw.    Electric drill.
Scoops.    Shovels.    Forks.
Sand bucket.    Wooden lathe.
Clipper fanning mill.
Gas motor with power jack.
Extension ladder.    Tarp.
Heat houser for Ford and John Deere tractors.
Fencing tools.    Emery stand.
Steel post driver.    Limb saw.
New hand seeder.    Sled.
U.S. Standard steel platform scale.
Metal calf creep feeder.
19 Crossote posts.    Barb wire.
Approximately 50 steel posts.
Some smooth wire.    Pipe vise.
Pump jack with electric motor.
Electric fencers.    Buzz saw blade.
Set tractor chains.    Pipe vise.
Bench vise.    Cattle oiler.
Grease guns and cans.    4 Feed bunks.
Cattle squeeze chute.    Tank heater.

### HAY

Approximately 700 bales alfalfa, round bales.

TERMS: Cash. Nothing removed until settled for. Not responsible in case of an accident

# A. C. McCall Estate, Owners

### PAULINE KOON, ADMINISTRATRIX

FREDDIE KOLB AUCTION SERVICE.                         BILL MOUNTFORD AGENCY, CLERKS.
AUCTIONEER AND COMPLETE SALE SERVICE.

# Nebraska Farm Life
# WWI to WWII

*Malvern C. McCall*
*Pauline McCall Koon*
*Allan L. McCall*
*Richard C. McCall*

*Richard C. McCall, Editor.*

Writer's Showcase
San Jose New York Lincoln Shanghai

# Nebraska Farm Life WWI to WWII

Writer's Showcase
an imprint of iUniverse, Inc.

For information address:
iUniverse, Inc.
5220 S. 16th St., Suite 200
Lincoln, NE 68512
www.iuniverse.com

ISBN: 0-595-22760-0

Printed in the United States of America

*This book is dedicated to the memory of our parents, Mabel and Cecil McCall who brought us up with love and instilled into us the principles with which we have lived our lives.*

*Probable nor'east to sou'west winds, varying to the southard and westard and eastard and points between; high and low barometer, sweeping round from place to place; probable areas of rain, snow, hail, and drought, succeeded or preceded by earthquakes with thunder and lightning.*

—Mark Twain

# *Contents*

# *Foreword*

This is a book about a family growing up on the Republican River in south central Nebraska during the first half of the twentieth century. We all grew up doing farm work, and fishing and swimming in the Republican River were a major part of our entertainment. We all attended District 9 country school and then went to Red Cloud High School. This was a way of life that vanished soon after the youngest of us graduated. Younger people have seemed to be fascinated with the stories that we tell about this period, and we decided that some of it should be written down. From our various perspectives, the four surviving siblings discuss family life on the farm, the economics of the time, the medical and veterinary practices, country school education, and social life. Some of it is serious and some of it is more or less funny anecdotes. Our sister was a country schoolteacher and had many memories of country school. One of our brothers is a physician and was particularly interested in the medical practices of the day, as well as the state of veterinary medicine. The youngest of us transcribed tapes from the others and edited the results, with large amounts of assistance from the others.

# *Acknowledgements*

The editor is grateful for the help he has received from many people in preparing this manuscript. He especially wishes to thank Mary McCall and Lela Kelliher for proofreading and correcting his sometimes shaky grammar. His son, James, provided assistance with computer technicalities.

# List of Contributors

The Webster County Museum kindly allowed us to remove a photograph of the Mount Pleasant Church from their display so that it could be scanned.

# 1

## *The Town*

The stories in this book all took place in or near the little town of Red Cloud, Nebraska and the even smaller village of Inavale, Nebraska. Red Cloud is on the Republican River, just a few miles from the Kansas State line and in the middle of the state east and west. We grew up on a farm across the river from Red Cloud. We were about 7 miles from Red Cloud and 4 miles from Inavale. Red Cloud was named after the Sioux chief who supposedly had a village nearby at one time.

Red Cloud was settled in 1870 by Silas Garber, later governor of Nebraska, and a few others. It was first known as the Upper Stockade. (The Lower Stockade became Guide Rock.) More settlers arrived in 1871, including our grandfather, Alfred C. McCall, and his brother, Oliver. A well-known settler that arrived in 1870 was a parrot that spoke only Spanish when it arrived but later converted to English. It is duly recorded that it died in 1890. The town was later incorporated as Red Cloud and by 1890 it had a population of 2448. Red Cloud is in Webster County, which is 24 miles square, and which had a population of nearly 7000 by 1879. The populations of both the town and county are much smaller now. The county showed a surprising dedication to education, with three school districts formed in the county in 1871. By 1890 there were 75 school districts, 67 of which had schoolhouses.

Old-timers told us that at one time Red Cloud had been an important cattle-shipping center and had had a population of about 5000. However, by our time, it had shrunk to a population of about 1700 and few trains ran on the railroad tracks that passed on the south side of town. The town's function was to serve the surrounding farms. It had a library, three grocery stores, a movie theater, a couple of restaurants, hardware stores, drugstores (one with a soda fountain), clothing stores, a bank, etc. The big days were Tuesday afternoon, when there was a livestock sale, and Saturday night, when all the farmers came to town for shopping and socializing.

Saturday night was a really busy night and parking was at a premium. The sidewalks on the two business blocks were packed with people. The farm wives did their week's shopping and stood gossiping in groups. The men hung out in or outside the two poolhalls, which were really more beer joints with a few pool tables. There were no bars and nice women did not go into the poolhalls. The farm kids went to the library and the movie theatre, which usually had a double bill on Saturday. Of course, you had to have a dime for admission and it was nice if you had a nickel for popcorn. We were fortunate because we sold firewood to the theatre owner, who paid us off in movie admissions. After the movie, the kids ran wildly through the crowds trying to stay out of sight of their parents, in order to go home as late as possible. On occasion a rainstorm came up during the evening and the parents made a mad search to find the kids and go home. Virtually all of the farms were on dirt roads, some of which were clay, and they quickly became impassible with heavy rain. We always felt that if we got over the "big hill" we could make it the rest of the way. When we were small, we really felt that it was a big hill, but it must have shrunk because it is not much of a hill now. However, it was in a clay area and got very slick very quickly when it rained. It was not that uncommon to have to go to the nearest neighbor and get him to come and pull us up the hill with his team or in later years, his tractor.

It was a pleasant little town with friendly people. On hot summer evenings, people sat on their front porches or strolled along the streets. The strollers stopped and talked to the porch sitters and the porch sitters sat and talked about the strollers. Beyond the movies, which changed three times per week, there was not a great deal of entertainment. The churches were active (there were at least eight churches plus a vacant one used by travelling evangelists) and high school sports events and plays were well attended. On the Fourth of July, there was usually a parade, and families had picnics in the park with fireworks east of town in the evening. The fireworks were held in our uncle's pasture and often resulted in a grass fire, so they were quite exciting. Beyond these organized activities, people made their own entertainment: playing cards, listening to the radio, hunting and fishing and having friends for dinner.

Red Cloud's chief claim to fame is that it was the home of the novelist Willa Cather when she was growing up. The Cather museum and tour attract a certain number of tourist visits. Our mother remembered sitting on Cather's lap when she was small. She was not completely popular in Red Cloud since she wrote about some thinly disguised families in the area and they did not like her descriptions of some events.

The high school was larger than you would expect because it drew farm kids from a large area around the town. Most of them went to one-room country schools through the eighth grade and then went to town for high school. There were no school buses, so the farm kids either had to drive or board with a family that lived in Red Cloud. Nebraska allowed kids to get a school permit when they were 12 years old. In theory, this allowed you to drive to school and back home by the shortest route. In practice, the kids stretched this to the limit. There was surprisingly little wild driving. This may in part be due to the fact that the cars the kids drove were usually tired old wrecks that had been discarded by their fathers. The kids who boarded in town mainly worked for their landlord to pay for part of their board and room. Since we had lots of relatives, we all boarded with relatives during our high school years.

The quality of the teaching was very variable. We had some old teachers who had been there for many years, two or three of whom had taught our mother and were still there to teach most of us. We considered most of them "mean" but, in general, they were the best of the teachers. Stella Ducker, Jessie Kellogg and Florence Kellogg were prominent among this group. The rest of the teachers came and left again after two or three years. During World War II, the teaching was particularly bad since many of the male teachers had been drafted. In order to get teachers at all, the school was forced to hire teachers who had retired or were teaching on permits because they lacked the qualifications to teach these subjects. Overall, the education was good enough that most kids who wanted to go to college were able to get into a school that they wanted.

Now things have changed dramatically from the time of our childhood. The town has shrunk down to about 1300. Of those 1300, an amazing number are widows, mostly of farmers, who have moved to town after the death of their husbands. Better roads and better cars allow people to go to Hastings or Grand Island to shop, and many of the stores in Red Cloud have closed. Television ended the little movie theatre. On Saturday night now, the downtown area is totally deserted, without a car or person in sight and no stores open. Few sit out on their porches on hot summer evenings since most of them are inside watching television in their air-conditioned living rooms. While there are now a few joggers, there are rarely strollers. The lack of jobs means that most of the young people leave town after graduation from high school.

# 2

# *The Family*

## Our Parents' Generation

Our parents, Cecil Monti McCall and Mabel Emma (Bradshaw) McCall, were married in 1906 and produced the five of us over the period 1907 to 1929. Alfred (Alf), the oldest, farmed part of the family farm and died in 1972. The rest of us are still alive and this book is based upon our collective recollections. Except for Alf and Polly, the

Mabel and Cecil McCall, ca. 1946

rest of us left the area and lived in various parts of the country, as well as in Germany and Sweden during our active lives. All of us married people born and brought up in Red Cloud or nearby towns except Dick. Dick married Mary Gregory, who was brought up on Long

Island. There were ten grandchildren and a growing number of great grandchildren.

Dad was born in 1881, the son of a farmer and banker in the area, who had come to Nebraska from Pennsylvania and produced a family of 11 children by his first wife and one by his second wife. Mom was the youngest of a large family of English immigrants and was one of the three children out of nine who were born in this country near Red Cloud. They were married in 1906 when Mom was just over 17 years old. They had wanted to be married the previous year but her mother thought that 16 was too young to get married.

The Saturday after their June wedding they went into Red Cloud and bought the finest buggy that was available in town. Afterwards, Dad told Mom to go do the grocery shopping for the week. She said that she would have to have some money and was shocked to hear him say they would have to charge it since they would have no more money until after the fall harvest. She took over a household that had one of Dad's brothers and several hired men to cook for, all of whom loved to tease this young bride. It must have been difficult but she never spoke of it except with humor.

Dad had only an eighth-grade education and worked as a tinsmith and a schoolteacher before he settled into the life of a farmer. He was a staunch Republican and one of his major regrets was that he had been persuaded to vote for Roosevelt for his first term. His other major regret was that his parents would not give him permission to join the army during the Spanish American War. (Dick took advantage of this when he needed permission to join the army at 17 toward the end of World War II). He was a stubborn man, a trait the rest of us have also been accused of. He never accepted Daylight Saving Time, which he called Roosevelt Time. He never changed his watch during the year. He was not a very demonstrative man except toward Mom but we never had any doubt of his love and support. He expected a lot out of us and seldom complimented us on the result of a job well done, which was what he had expected. On the other hand, he was tolerant of our

occasional misdeeds. Most of us can remember only one or two spank-
ings when we were growing up. Dad was a good farmer and suffered
less than most when the drought hit in the '30's. However, there came
a time when the mortgage was so high that he told the mortgage company to take the farm. Fortunately, so many farms had been taken that
they did not want it and chose to carry him. After the end of the
drought and the recovery of the economy in World War II, he prospered again and the farm was free and clear at his death.

Mom had some high school, but we do not think that she graduated. She went directly to keeping house for Dad, several of his brothers, and several hired men. It could not have been easy for her since her
cooking was apparently not the most skillful. However, she managed
and eventually became a very good plain cook and baker. She was often
asked to make wedding cakes for local weddings and had a set of pans
for making tiered angel food cakes. After the birth of the youngest of
us, Dick, her health deteriorated. She was eventually taken to the Mayo
Clinic and diagnosed as having Pott's disease (tuberculosis of the
spine). Mom was an early recipient of an operation where bone from
the leg was used to replace diseased bone in the spine. There was a long
and painful recovery with months of wearing a heavy brace and not
being able to get out of bed without Dad's help. While she loved to
talk about her ailments, it was never in a complaining way. She probably suffered from back pain most of her life after that but seldom mentioned it. Mom loved to talk and wherever she went she struck up a
conversation with whoever was nearby. She visited Dick one time
when he was living in the Boston area. After her visit in Boston, she
flew to California to visit Allan. She was talking to the man sitting
beside her and told him where she was from and that she thought they
would fly quite close to there on their way to California. He mentioned
it to the stewardess, who asked the pilot. A few hours later the pilot
announced over the speaker system that they were now flying over Red
Cloud, Nebraska, which must have mystified most of the passengers.
Mom was convinced that she had seen the farm house and that the

pilot had detoured to please her, and she wrote a letter to United Airlines commending him for his politeness. We do not know what United said to the pilot but they sent Mom a nice letter saying they were pleased to have made her day.

Since we lived on a dirt road that was often impassible due to mud or snow, it was sometimes not possible to get a doctor when needed. Mom was often called upon in such cases, and she delivered several babies.

She usually deferred to Dad's decisions but on occasion she thought he was wrong. In those cases, it was always done the way Mom wanted it. They seemed to have a real loving marriage and had worked out all the conflicts, as far as we kids knew.

The old house we lived in then was getting pretty old. It was probably built for Dad's Uncle Oliver about 1880 or 1890. None of the buildings built during those early years lasted very long because they did not have cement for foundations. That area had no solid rock so they used layers of soft chalky rock from nearby and laid them on the ground for a foundation. The soil was loose and the rock crumbled and sank into the ground over the years. Many years later, cement was brought in and somebody near Red Cloud started making bricks of fairly good quality. The lumber used to build the old house was hauled 60 miles from the nearest railroad by teams and wagons. Dad and Uncle Mal decided to build a new house. They visited new houses in two counties to get ideas. It was to be a modern house with running water and it was even wired for electricity, although there were no power lines on our (south) side of the Republican River. It had a full concrete basement with three floors above, including four bedrooms upstairs, as well as a room with windows all around two sides that we called a sleeping porch and one bedroom downstairs, and a big kitchen, family room and parlor. All of the first floor had oak floors and built-in oak cabinets. The house was finished in late 1919 or 1920. It was heated with a big convection hot-air furnace that burned logs.

The new Cecil McCall house soon after it was built. The old house is
seen on the left.

The firebox was big enough that a man could lie in it. The only
wood that we had was cottonwood and box elder that was not really
very good wood for heating. It used so much wood that it took lot of
labor to provide an adequate supply. In the summer, we would cut
down trees and just leave them there to dry out. On winter days when
it was too cold to do anything else, we would saw them up in furnace
lengths, about five to six feet, split the bigger logs and haul them into
the basement by the furnace. In spite of its size, it was not adequate to
heat the whole house and the hot air registers in the upstairs bedrooms
were always closed.

The warmest room in the house was always the kitchen, which got a
lot of heat from the big old Majestic wood range. There was a fire in it
from morning until after the evening dinner. This burned short
lengths of wood and corncobs and it was the duty of the smallest boy
to keep the wood and cob boxes filled. Corncobs burn fast and hot and
Mom could control the temperature of the stove and the oven by toss-
ing in cobs a few at a time. On bitter cold winter days, when you came
in to warm your frozen feet, it was wonderful to open the oven and
stick your feet inside.

Dad and three other farmers went together to put in a power line, transformers and other necessities to bring electrical power to the farms. Theirs were the first farms in the area to have electric lights and soon had washing machines, electric refrigerators, other small appliances, and electric motors to pump water into their homes. There was telephone service even before the war but the farmers who broke the line had to repair it the best they could. Sometimes the poles had rotted and fallen in a windstorm and they fastened the single wire to the fence post. We had a wooden telephone box on the wall, with a crank on the side, which we used to ring our neighbors or the central office in Red Cloud where they could connect us with other lines or cities. Each phone had a ring, which was sounded in long and short rings, e.g., one long, one short and one long, which told you that someone wanted to talk to you. Our ring was two longs. Some subscribers were a little nosy and would listen in on other people's conversations. Sometimes there was a quick series of about six rings, called a line call, which asked for everybody's attention. Everybody listened and there would be an announcement. Usually, it was something like "On Thursday morning there will be a carload of cabbage (or apples or potatoes) at the railroad station in Red Cloud," so that the farmers could go in there and stock up. Sometimes also the line call might be a call for help, such as for a prairie fire or a burning house.

Dad and his brother Mal were partners from their early twenties. They initially were on their father's farm and then they bought their Uncle Oliver's farm of about 200 acres, which had some river-bottom land. They prospered on this land and were able to buy other land later. They followed our granddad's path of feeding cattle and hogs and growing corn and alfalfa and other kinds of hay and fodder with which to feed them. Usually the profit was good. Mal suffered from epilepsy from the age of 19 until his death at age 50 and never married. Sometimes, the seizures came often and were violent at times. He never knew when they were coming, and if it was a mild one, he might not know afterwards that it had happened. It did not affect his mind. He was a shrewd judge of cattle and would give the seller a price per pound or a price per head, whichever the seller preferred. He could mentally price them by guessing their weight, which we could later check on our big farm scales. It was uncanny how close the price per pound would come to what he had based his offer upon, even though he had not graduated from the country school. He spent a small fortune in hospital and doctor bills in hopes of curing his disease but nothing worked and his seizures became more frequent and more serious.

The first treatment he heard about was in Cincinnati. He got George Jensen, a neighbor who had just gotten back from the war, to go with him. Dad told George to have a good time and that Mal had plenty of money to pay for it. They went back there and Mal had some sort of abdominal surgery—we don't know just what. He was gone for more than a month, maybe two, and when he came home they had him lie on a board on the bed with the foot end raised up about two feet above his head. He had to do that every day after a meal and stay there for about an hour. They had told him that his internal organs were all out of place and that they had shifted them around. He couldn't walk around or do much of anything for another month. That cost about $4000, which was a lot of money in those days. It did not help one bit and the seizures started right in again.

Another of his many treatments involved a visit to Waconda Springs in Kansas where he took mineral waters for his treatment. For many years he lived with us, and Dad and Mother were constantly watching him. He did have some falls and injuries but never hurt any of us. Mom and Dad were always afraid that he would injure one of us in a seizure because we loved him and he liked us and we always wanted to be near him. Finally, he went to live on his farm with his brother, John. He finally died from a violent seizure, from which he never recovered. When he died, Dad bought Mal's share in the partnership.

When Dad was growing up, there was a lot of land that was open range. They had more cattle than they could graze on their own pasture so Dad, riding a horse, would take a herd of cattle out to the open range and spend a day while they ate grass. On the way he would go by a neighbor's, an old bachelor, who lived in a little house. Sometimes it was cold and Dad would stop there to get warm or to get a drink. The old fellow liked to play cards so he taught Dad how to play. Dad would stop in every once in a while and have a game or two. Dad's two older sisters, Mildred and Martha, were taking care of the household since their mother had died. Dad had gone to town and bought a deck of cards. One day he left the cards in his pocket and his sisters found them when they went to wash the clothes. They thought that cards were the devil's game and they were astounded that he would have a deck of cards in his pocket. Granddad came home and they told him and showed him the cards. They said Just think, this young boy had those playing cards. They said, We will take care of the cards and you take care of him. Granddad said he would and talked to Dad, who admitted that he had them.

"Where did you get them?"

"I bought them in town."

"Where did you learn to play cards?"

"From old man (somebody) up on the hill."

"What kind of cards did you play?"

We do not know what kind of card game they played. Granddad asked him if he was a pretty good player. Dad said he was pretty good and had played quite a few times. Granddad said, Well, let's go have a game."

In later years, cards became a favorite type of recreation for our family. All of us kids would play rummy with Dad if he was in the house. Among ourselves, cribbage was a popular game. The older kids also played cribbage with our maternal grandmother, who stayed with us sometimes. She loved to play but would never play on Sunday. One snowy Sunday when nobody could go to church, she forgot that it was Sunday and played cribbage with Mal. She was horrified when she realized that she had broken the Sabbath. Often in the evenings the family would choose up sides and play games like pitch or a variation of it called high five. We would sometimes have apples or popcorn for a special treat.

Of Dad's brothers, John was the one we saw most of because he came and worked for us fairly frequently. John was the youngest son in our Dad's family and he was maybe six years old or a little more when his mother died. The two older sisters, Martha and Mildred, took over the household duties and took care of their father and John. Most of his siblings had left home by the time he was a teenager, and had their own farms or businesses. John did not learn very fast as far as school went, and as he grew up, they began to suspect that there was something wrong with him. He didn't have a very good life with all of these older sisters and brothers. Anyway, he grew up and went to school a little bit at least. We know that he could read and write but probably not very well. He would try to go to work for somebody but he was not responsible enough to do a good job. Like Topsy, he just grew. A couple times he and another bachelor would live together for a while. He never could really make it on his own. When our Uncle Mal died, he knew John needed some help, and he made some arrangements for him. We are uncertain just how he did it. John got quite a bit of money from Mal's estate and he had also inherited money from his father. He didn't know how to handle it, of course, and they chose Lawrence, the oldest son, to be his guardian. Uncle Lawrence would give him money for what he needed and try to get him to help himself as much as he could. Later, Dad took over the guardianship and, when his health began to fail, Aunt Mildred took over in turn. She found out that it was not such an easy job and finally she took John into one of her tenant houses to live. She was a widow by that time. He lived with her for some time. About the only duty she got out of him was that he could drive a car and she could not. They got along pretty well, but finally as he got older, he got to be more helpless. He still had a little money left over. He had never married. His money was divided up equally among his surviving brothers and sisters and his many nieces and nephews. He had lived exactly as he wanted to live and worked no more than he felt like his entire life.

Our home was nice and it was instilled in us that we should have pride in our home and do what was necessary to keep it nice. Our dad always mowed the weeds along the road because he thought it made the place look better and it made the road safer too. He was also one of the first in the area to build dams. He built little brush dams in erosion spots and larger dams to hold rain runoff water. Some of these are still holding water in the pastures. The work was done mostly by mules and little graders. We had two—a larger one that we pulled with four mules and called a Fresno and a smaller one that we pulled with two mules that we called the slip. We burned wood to heat the house and to cook and that also kept up the place by burning the fallen trees and branches. Dad was a conservationist. He believed in and practiced soil conservation and crop rotation. He did a lot of public service. The water supply at our country school was a cistern that collected rainwater from the roof. Each year it had to be emptied and cleaned out, and one year there was no rain after the cleaning, so the school had no water. We always wondered if it was really safe to drink, but it was delightful to wash your hands in that soft rainwater. Dad hauled a five-gallon jug of water to school every day so that the kids could at least have a drink during the day. While he did not attend church, he would go to the church at 8 o'clock on cold mornings and start a fire in the stove, take up a load of wood in the car, stoke it up, come back in an hour and put in more fuel. At the time for Sunday school he would take us all to the church, with more wood for the fire. He kept the Lord's house warm more by his duties than the rest of us did with all the praying we did.

## Our Generation

There were five of us children. Alfred (Alf) was born in 1907, followed by Malvern (Mal) in 1912, Pauline (Polly) in1915, Allan (Mac) in 1924 and Richard (Dick) in 1929. This very spread-out family spanned almost two generations. Alf stayed in the area and farmed part of Dad's farm all of his life. He died in 1972 and is survived by two daughters and several grandchildren and great grandchildren.

The McCall Family—ca. 1941. From left to right, Allan, Dick, Polly, Dad, Mom, Alf and Mal

We think a few words at this time about Alf would be appropriate. He, of course, does not have the opportunity to introduce anything here. Allan was probably as close to Alf as any others in the family, with the exception of Polly. Allan's last few summers before he left home were spent working for him. Our father by this time was old enough that he hadn't a lot of interest in doing much of the farm work himself other than supervising and managing. Allan worked for Alf not only in tending the separator but also in the ensilage-cutting business. During those times, Alf was really more of a father to him than his father was and many people asked and thought that perhaps he was his father. On several occasions when he had a father-son banquet at the high school, Alf would volunteer to be a father and always seemed to enjoy it. He was quite an intelligent, innovative fellow and was a classic example of an under-achiever. In the early days, he taught himself radio and in later years in addition to his skills at farming he taught himself how to weld electrically and was quite an expert on motors. Allan helped him several times when he would overhaul his car and the old Case tractor. The Case tractor came with steel "tiptoe" lugs which shook you to pieces on hard ground and were not much better than rubber tires for traction. Dick watched him convert to rubber tires once when he was visiting at home. This involved cutting off all the steel strap spokes in the wheels with a hacksaw and then welding on a new rim for the rubber tire. He had very little in the way of measuring tools except a steel tape, which Dick thought was grossly inadequate. However, when he had the old rim cut off, Dick helped him lift the new rim in place and it fit beautifully. Alf was quite inventive, and his farm was full of clever gadgets that he had made. He and Allan's wife, Peggy, became fond of one another and whenever Allan came home from the university or army days, they would often share his home and food. It was a very sad time for them when he came to visit them when he was terminal in his carcinomatosis. At that time, there was nothing they could do for him. It was remarkable that at his retirement at age 65, he applied for Social Security and collected only two checks before his demise. Allan and Peggy had had a similar unhappy time earlier when his wife, Lucille, came to visit them in a similar state with terminal carcinomatosis. Again, there was nothing they could do for her. It was a fitting tribute to Alf that on the day of his funeral, we afterwards gathered at Polly's home and emptied and consumed the remains of his liquor stock. We remarked at that time that he was probably looking down kindly upon us.

Mal tried farming for a couple years and was defeated by grasshoppers and Nebraska weather. He went to California in 1935 and did various things, including working in the orange groves of a cousin. During WWII, he was trained as a machinist and worked at this trade in California and Washington the rest of his career. Eventually, he became production foreman in a radiator-manufacturing plant. Here his high school Spanish, honed by his years in the orange groves, proved useful and he was sent to Mexico and Argentina to assist in getting new radiator plants in operation. He retired early and spent several years travelling around the country with his wife, Myrl. At one time, he came to Northern California and worked for some time in the same laboratory where Dick worked. This was great for Dick, since Mal had left home when Dick was five years old and he did not really know him very well.

Polly was a country schoolteacher for six years before her marriage to William Koon. Except for several years during WWII when she accompanied her husband in his navy service, she has remained in the Red Cloud area all of her life.

Allan went to the University of Nebraska for two years and then enlisted in the army after WWII broke out. While he was in the service, the army sent him to medical school at the University of Utah, and he completed this after his discharge. He then re-enlisted for the Korean police action and spent most of his time in Germany with the occupation forces. Upon his discharge, he took up practice in Redlands, CA, and has remained there until the present.

Dick enlisted in the army after completing high school and spent almost all of his time in Korea in the occupation forces. After his discharge, he attended the Massachusetts Institute of Technology where he received his Bachelor of Science and Ph.D. degrees in physics. He worked in Washington at the Hanford Project, two years in Sweden on a research fellowship, three years for a company in Boston, and then at the Stanford Linear Accelerator Center for 27 years. He also worked as a consultant and is just now finishing his final project.

Allan belonged to the Future Farmers of America during high school. This required him to have a project that was farm-related every year. One year he had turkeys. There were about 100 of them that spent the night in a portable coop that he had placed by a haystack in the middle of an alfalfa field. The birds were too stupid ever to learn that they were supposed to go there at the end of the day so Allan with Dick's unwilling help had to drive them out there. As the alfalfa got taller, this became harder and harder. The turkeys would get sidetracked in pursuit of a grasshopper and we would arrive at the shed and find we were missing a few. These would have to be searched out one by one and driven or carried to the coop. Another of his projects, which he had several years, was sheep. They were in a small pasture, which did not have a very good fence, and was across the road from the house. We had particularly heavy rains one year and the fence kept being washed out, allowing the sheep to escape. Allan was living in town during the week to go to high school so Dick was stuck with repairing the fence. He was marginally old enough to do this and the job was complicated by the presence of a borrowed ram. If he let his attention stray for a minute, the ram would butt him into the fence. Probably his dislike for farming was solidified by those blasted sheep.

Mal was born June 12, 1912 on the farm, as were all of us, and since Alf died, he is the patriarch of this family. The earliest event that he can remember is the birth of Polly and he did not understand it much except that he had a baby sister. We have a picture of the old farmhouse and Polly and Mal are standing out in front. It looks like Mal was five and she was three. The old house was in front of the present house and closer to the road.

The next thing Mal remembers is the flu epidemic of 1918 and later. The three or four town doctors were working day and night, making house calls in town and in the country. Dad had gone to Kansas City with a load of cattle, and everybody got sick. We think both Alf and Mal got it. The hired man left because he was afraid of it. Our Uncle Mal and his man came down to feed our cattle and both of them got so sick that Mom fixed beds for them and tried to take care of all of them. Although there were quite a few deaths in the area, all of her patients survived and Dad was back in three days. Soon after that, WWI ended, and Mal remembers some of the area's soldiers coming home. The little town of Inavale, population 150 at that time, put on a big barbecue to celebrate the armistice. They had a huge iron kettle, which they filled with several hundred pounds of beef, and cooked it all night with vegetables. The next day all of the families from miles around came. There were games for the kids, ballgames, and it was a happy crowd. They served everybody beef on big buns and tin cups of soup. It was so great that Inavale did it for several years on Armistice Day.

As Alf had done before him, Mal attended Red Cloud High School, and graduated in 1929 in a class of 32 students. In 1929, the farming and cattle business was making a lot of money and he could have gone to the University of Nebraska at Lincoln. However, he liked farming and chose to go to work with Dad. About that time, Alf took over about half of the land and formed a partnership with Dad but continued to live at home until he married a farm girl a few years later.

There are many stories about Christmases. The first Christmas that Mal can remember was when he was about four years old. The main thing he can remember on that Christmas was a tin horn that made quite a blast. He thought it was a great present so he blew it a few times while he was in the house and the rest of the people didn't like that much. Then he went outside down towards the feedlots and blew it. The cattle were scared and stampeded in a bunch to the far end of the lot. Luckily, they stopped at the fence a few hundred yards away. Dad didn't like having those fat cattle running like that, so he couldn't blow it in the house and couldn't blow it outside, and he didn't get much use out of it.

This brings back the memories of Christmas coming and Mother's preparations. It was a big thing in our family, and soon after Thanksgiving Mother would start preparing candies and special foods for Christmas. There was a little closet off the hall between the kitchen and the front door. It had a bunch of shelves and she would start putting Christmas things in there. She made Christmas candy that would keep well and she made quite a variety. She made taffy and fudge and divinity, butterscotch, stuffed dates, and several different kinds of cookies. One thing that everybody liked were popcorn balls. She made the popcorn balls big enough that you could hold them in your hand and eat. They were stuck together with a butterscotch type of syrup and they were really good. We think about them but most of us have never made them. We usually had nice gift at Christmas. We usually had a Christmas tree. One of the first things Allan remembers is Dad taking him to cut a Christmas tree. There was a place a mile or two up in the hills where there had once been a house. The house was gone, but they had planted some cedar trees. Dad took him when he was maybe five years old. There was snow on the ground and it was quite a walk for him. Dad cut some branches from the trees and tied them together and made a Christmas tree. That was the kind of tree we had every year but that was the first time he had ever seen it done. They dragged the branches through the snow back home and everybody helped wire them together to make a tree. This did not make a very pretty tree but it smelled wonderful. Usually everyone had one special gift, and there were a lot of little things on the tree. We used to put popcorn strings on the tree and the little kids made paper chains. One memorable gift Mal got was an air rifle. In later years, Allan also got an air rifle. After a while he went outside to try it and shot at a sparrow up in a tree. He hit it and killed it and came in the house, crying and saying he didn't mean to kill it. One year quite a few years later, Mal got a .22 rifle and that was a big gift for him. It was kind of a cheapy—a single-shot bolt action and, although it was a nice rifle, you had to stop and reload it every time you shot. He enjoyed that for years and later on traded it for a different gun for hunting and traded that for a revolver. It wasn't much good either.

There was one year that Dick really wanted a sled for Christmas. Money was very tight and Alf went out to the city dump and found a sled, which he fixed up for him. The part of one runner where it curves up to the top of the sled was broken off and missing. Alf replaced it with a piece from some farm machinery, which was a round rod with a clevis at one end that he used to bolt on to the straight part of the runner. He painted it bright red and Dick was delighted with it. He immediately spotted the repair joint and wanted to know what that was. When told it was a shock absorber, he was even more proud of his sled, since it was the only one he had ever seen with a shock absorber.

Dad always did his Christmas shopping on Christmas Eve. He would disappear into his office and come out with a bundle of white envelopes, which he would place on the tree. Each one had a name on it and contained a sum of money, which varied, depending on the age of the child. Mom worried every year that one or more of the envelopes would get mixed up with the discarded wrapping paper and be lost. We all laughed at her but most years at least one of them would be lost and require a search.

We had our Christmas tree in the morning but we had to have breakfast first. After eating breakfast, there was no restriction on our eating candy or cookies. Breakfast was always big, with bacon, eggs, fried potatoes and grapefruit. For the smallest children it seemed to take an eternity to eat. After breakfast was finally over, we moved into the living room and the smallest child who could read names handed out the presents. In later, leaner years, we five children drew names rather than getting presents for all of our siblings. In retrospect, they were quite meager Christmases compared to the riches that our children and grandchildren have. To us kids, however, it always seemed like a wonderful Christmas with loads of good things. We always had one big toy, usually selected after much poring over the Sears and Montgomery Ward catalogs. In addition there were smaller presents that always included one or two books.

The family social life was heavily based on having guests for a meal. Since our house on the farm was large, there was always room for extra people and our parents always welcomed guests. Both sides of the family, our Dad's side, and Mom's side, the Bradshaws, were clannish people and at a drop of the hat there were reunions. It seemed like the reunions were always at our house. Our mother always enjoyed guests, there was always plenty of food, and everyone seemed to have a good time. Sometimes, the excuse for a get-together was when we had something special to eat that we wanted to share. On occasion, we would catch an unusually large number of fish. At these times, we would invite some relatives to come out for a fish fry. One time, Allan and

Dick went fishing in one of the flood ponds left from the 1935 flood. There had evidently been a population explosion of bullheads and they brought home about all they could carry. They and Mom spent hours dressing all those little fish and we had some relatives out for supper the next day. The bullheads were small but delicious when fried, more like trout than catfish.

The biggest occasion in the year was our grandmother Bradshaw's birthday. She was an English lady and had been through some hard times after she came from England. She had raised a large family and all of her children except one were within a close distance to where we lived. Grandfather died when Mom was just a child and Grandmother lived with us most of the year but spent the summer months with our Aunt Sophie. It seemed that this was the time of the year that she needed a cooler, modern house, which Aunt Sophie did not have, and we did, but she always seemed happy to go to Aunt Sophie. Her birthday was in April and that was the time when it was planned that all of the relatives would come to our house and celebrate Grandmother's birthday. Grandmother had a sister who had as large a family as Grandmother did, and they were always included in the invitation to the birthday party. Each family brought something—usually, the thing that they were best known for. However, if you saw the preparations at our house, you would think that nobody was bringing anything: Mother would cook several chickens, a big piece of Dad's corned beef, half of a ham, pies and cakes. Everybody else brought as lavishly, so there was an abundance of food. People came through the morning and usually we set out the spread and ate about one o'clock. We made no attempt to seat this many people. Our porch had a wide railing and people would put their food and drinks on the railing and line up there like cows at a manger. Nobody minded standing at the manger for that length of time. We had a wide front stairs and many people sat on the stairs to eat. It was a pleasant time and the attendance varied from 50 to 75. As kids, we all loved it because we got to see cousins whom we did not see very often. It was something that Grandmother looked forward to all year. A friend of hers from the time when they first came from England, who was a schoolteacher, was always invited, and she always brought Grandmother a five-dollar gold piece for a present. There was always a beautiful birthday cake. Our mother usually made angel food cakes and once she and another lady made a three-layer cake, which was quite a sensation. It was a lot of work, since our mother was a good housekeeper and she wanted the whole house clean. People migrated upstairs and through the whole house, and every room had to be presentable. Afterwards, there was usually a huge mess where food had been spilled and there were usually some babies that had accidents. It was a very mixed crowd but somehow they all got along together.

Also, we had family dinners for Dad's side of the family when somebody was visiting or there was a special birthday or a marriage. Again, they usually congregated at our house. Sometimes, it was impromptu and it wasn't as much work, since we didn't have time to clean out closets, dust the tops of windows, and other cleaning chores that were not done that often. One time our aunt and two of her daughters had decided to go to California to live and we were giving a farewell party for them. It must have been spring, because we had been having nice weather, but that day a snowstorm came up and by the time dinner was over, it was really bad with blowing snow. It wasn't very cold but very wet and disagreeable. We had a large group of people there and several families did not risk the roads and stayed at our house for the night. Several other families started home by way of Inavale, which they thought would be easier because of less drifting of the snow, and they got stranded with neighbors along the way. Two of the families stayed with neighbors with a small house who did not expect to have to feed that many people but they did the best they could for them. Our aunt, her daughter and her daughter's boyfriend thought they could get home but got stuck just a couple miles up the road. They were close to a house and phoned us. Dad and one of the boys hitched a team of mules to a wagon and brought them back to our house. Needless to say, they were very glad for the shelter. The boyfriend was quite cha-grined, since he thought he was a good driver and could get through. The party was on Sunday and it was Monday afternoon before the road was opened up and they could all get out, so we had an impromptu slumber party.

We always laughed at Mom's older brother, because whenever he came, he always brought a pound of coffee. He had a small grocery store so this was an easy thing for him to bring. However, we thought he must always carry a pound of coffee in his car, since even when he stopped in when driving by, he would still bring a pound of coffee. It got to be a joke because everybody just stood at the door when he came and waited for the pound of coffee. He and another of Mom's brothers had small grocery stores in small towns west of us. We kids always liked their visits because they would bring us a bag of candy. One always brought hard vanilla filled chocolates and the other would bring a bag of mixed candy.

# 3

## *The Country School*

All five of us went to the District 9 country school through the eighth grade. This was the typical one-room schoolhouse with a barn and boys' and girls' outhouses. It was one of the two newest schoolhouses in the county and was built during one of Mom's many terms on the schoolboard. Schools were built by the district itself with its allocation of property-tax money from the county property taxes. Mom was always proud of the fact that they built the new schoolhouse without a property tax increase and that it met the state standards for country schools. There was a playground that our dad would have mowed with a farm mower before school started. There were two see-saws, two swings and a chinning bar, although in the depression years there was seldom a rope on either of the swings. We usually had a ball and bat and a length of clothesline rope for jumping rope and tug of war. We had a fifteen-minute recess in the middle of the morning and afternoon and a half-hour lunch break. When the weather was passable, we rushed outside to play when excused and spent the absolute minimum time eating our lunches. We played baseball—-one-old-cat or workup—since there were never enough for two teams. "Handy over" over the barn was popular as was tag, pom-pom-pullaway, jail, New Orleans, steal sticks, and hide and seek. In the winter, fox-and-geese was first on the list when we had new snow. The girls played merry-go-round and quieter games, and the boys played rougher games. Mostly the girls played the rougher games, too. Usually, our ball was a softball and it was in bad shape. Once, we also had a volley-ball. None of us had ever seen volleyball played or knew how it was played but we used it to play keepaway. We also played shinny, a version of hockey without ice. We used a tin can instead of a puck, and sticks we cut from tree branches. We ended up frequently with skinned-up shins, black eyes and other injuries when the can flew into the air and hit someone. We never had any really bad accidents. We were fortunate enough to have a basement in our school and on the really cold days we played some indoor games down there. None of us felt that we were really deprived of proper recreational opportunities.

The District 9 Schoolhouse

In the fall, the teacher would put together a program that consisted of dialogues, recitations, and songs accompanied by our old pump organ. Sometimes, somebody would be brought in to play the ukulele and sing. We had lunch with sandwiches, cakes, pies, and coffee and sold the lunch for a small amount. Part of that money was used to buy things for the playground. We don't remember that anything much was ever bought except for a football and maybe a new softball. Much of it was used to buy things for the school, mostly for the beginners and first grade. There was very little money available for supplies for the teacher to work with. We are sure that many of the teachers spent their own money buying things like construction paper and paints and things like that.

The box suppers were quite interesting. They were preceded by a program by the students and the teachers and attended by everyone in the neighborhood. People were jammed into the little schoolroom like sardines. One teacher was very attractive and had a beautiful singing voice. One night she sang *The Prisoner's Song* and when she came to the line, "I wish I had someone to love me...", all of the young bucks in the neighborhood chorused, "I will, let me, etc." She was very embarrassed but she was a very good teacher—one of our best. All of the girls and women brought boxes. Some of them were decorated lavishly and some of them were just plain shoeboxes with a bow. The teacher's box was the one that was sought after. It was the one that brought the most money because everybody in the district knew the teacher and admired her. Young men who knew the teacher would come from other districts and make a great effort to buy the teacher's box. The boxes were filled with goodies, usually sandwiches and cake, pie or cookies and most of them were quite lavish. Sometimes two girls would go together and make a box and it was sold as a double box. Usually, one fellow and his best friend would buy the double box.

The number of students in the school varied from more than twenty to only six the last year the youngest of us was there. Polly taught there for three years and had 23 students in all eight grades, including her two younger brothers. This was a very heavy teaching load. In addition to the usual teaching and grading papers, the teacher had to keep the school clean, build fires in the coal furnace, haul out ashes, help saddle and harness ponies after school, and supervise the playground. When it snowed, she also had to shovel paths to the two outhouses. Polly was fortunate in being able to live at home. Most teachers had to board with some local family, as did Polly in later years at other schools. It might seem that having little brothers as pupils would cause some problems. The first day Dick was in school it was explained that you could only get a drink (from the open bucket in the hall) at recess and noon hour. A few minutes later he asked to go get a drink. Polly reminded him of the rules but Dick, being an independent four-year-old, went to get a drink anyhow. Polly followed him out to the hall and told him to take his seat. Then he made his big mistake and threw the cup of water at her! Dick was very resentful of the consequent spanking and went home and complained to Dad. He then got the only spanking he remembers ever getting from Dad and it made Polly's look like a love pat. He was told to never again come home and complain about a teacher and he never did. Polly required the students, most of whom had known her for years, to call her Miss Polly, including her brothers. It was years before Dick got out of the habit of calling her Miss Polly.

We had good teachers in our rural school and we had some poor teachers. We were taught that the teacher was to be respected. Sometimes it was a little hard to respect them when it seemed the teacher didn't know much more than we did.

The one-room schools are almost a thing of the past now. The teachers were not very well trained and most of them started teaching directly from high school. Some of them took some summer-school courses at college after they started teaching. However, the education that you got there compared very favorably with that received in the towns. The class that was reciting moved up to the front of the room and by the time you were in the eighth grade, you were hearing that class for the eighth time and even the dullest students tended to learn the material. The teachers got some supervision in that the county school superintendent visited several times a year and observed their teaching. For us kids this was always an occasion since the superintendent always told us a story before she left. The country school kids also had to go to town and take tests towards the end of the seventh and eighth grades. These were state-prepared tests and passing out of the seventh and eighth grades depended on passing these tests. As a school system, it worked pretty well. The farm kids never had a problem when they went to town for high school and they provided more than their share of valedictorians.

There was a certain informality possible in such a system. In the worst blizzards, the teacher still had to get to school in case some half-frozen pupil showed up. Since some of the families had no telephone and the country lines were not very reliable for those who had them, school was never cancelled. Sometimes, the snow would start during the day and, if it looked bad, parents would start arriving during the afternoon to take their children home. As long as there was one child there, school continued and the teacher had to stay there. There was a telephone but it always had very weak batteries and was unreliable. Dick remembers one entire week when only he and one other pupil could get to school. Since they were in the same grade, classes were finished in the morning and they and the teacher played three-handed pinochle all afternoon.

During the years that Polly taught at District 9, it was the height of the depression. Most of the kids were ragged and some of them were not well fed. Some of them would bring lunches that had nothing but bread and lard (lard was one of the commodities on the federal program). Polly could not just give the children handouts, since there was a lot of pride involved, but she tried to make soup for lunch in the winter at least once a week. There was a kerosene stove in the basement and she would ask everyone to bring something—a potato, an onion, some milk, etc. From these offerings she would concoct soup, generously adding things she brought from home. Some of the kids came from families that were renting little hill farms, which would barely provide a living in the best years, and these were dry, bad years. We were fortunate that although Dad was primarily a corn and cattle farmer, he also believed in variety. We always had a big garden that provided lots of things for Mom to can. We usually raised plenty of potatoes and often watermelons and cantaloupe.

Polly went to the rural school for eight years followed by four years at the high school in Red Cloud. After she got her teacher's certificate, she taught six years in rural schools. The rural schools were much the same through the years. Our dad talked about going to a rural school in the same district where we went and it was not much different. The teacher was a little woman who was very shy. She had a bunch of big boys who went to school only in spurts and the discipline problem was terrible. They paid no attention to the poor little teacher at all. One day our grandfather was driving by the schoolhouse in a buggy and saw one of these boys climbing out the window. Grandfather stopped, grabbed the boy, switched him with the buggy whip and stuffed him back in the window. That was better discipline than most parents have over their kids today. Nowadays, the parent would have complained the teacher or our grandfather had abused the poor child.

The schoolhouse that the three older attended, had been built long before that. The year that it was built our aunt taught that school. Soon after Polly started high school, a new schoolhouse was built. Allan and Dick went to school in the new schoolhouse and the aunt's daughter was the first teacher in the new schoolhouse. Our father bought the old school building and moved it up on the hill over our farmhouse for housing for a married hired man. Many years later this rural school was closed and the new schoolhouse in its turn was bought and moved several miles to become housing. During this writing, the schoolhouse entered into its third incarnation. It is now the Owens Country Lodge, offered for rent to hunters, parties, family reunions, or other occasions. The school buildings all over the county were much the same. At one time, there were 70 school districts, so that no one was more than three miles from a school. Most of them were just shed like buildings with three or four windows on each side with a little anteroom built on for coats and lunchpails and such. The old schoolhouse was very cold. It was on a hill and faced the north and it seemed that every breeze found a crack. In hot weather it was stifling. Most of the schools had one long recitation bench, the teacher's desk up by the blackboard, and the students' desks in rows in back of that bench. The old schoolhouse had double desks with a shelf underneath for books.

They were not nailed to the floor. If you were lucky you got to sit beside a treasured friend. If you were not so lucky you had to sit beside somebody you hated or even sit with someone of the opposite sex, which was just as bad. Up until about the sixth or seventh grade, being forced to sit with a boy/girl was sheer punishment. However, along about the seventh or eighth grade, you kind of wished you would get to sit with one. There were always more boys than girls in our school, especially in earlier years. We had twin cousins who went to the same school. We would ride horseback and meet at the corner and ride with them. Each spring you knew that there would be new people in school and some that would be dropping out because there were a number of small hill farms, and people would rent these, live there for a year and move out, usually poorer than when they came. There were all kinds of people who came. Mostly, the kids were pretty well behaved. We had one teacher who came in when there had been no discipline at all the year before. We had some big boys who were very defiant. She was a little bit of a thing, maybe about 104 pounds, and 17 years old. She decided that she was going to make those kids behave. She got a short piece of rubber hose. One of the boys defied her and she really thrashed him with the rubber hose. One day something happened—we don't know what—and she lined up all of the boys and one by one she really worked them over with that rubber hose. And you know, not a single one of those kids ever defied her again. Several of them got whipped several times, but by the end of school year every one of those kids was eating out of her hand. The orneriest boy of them all waited after school to help her clean the schoolhouse, carried her books, and went out of his way to walk with her.

Quite a few of the kids rode a horse to school and a few drove a one-horse buggy. Often there would be two kids on the horse and one family had four kids on one horse. Frequently, the smallest child on the back would slip off going up what we called the "big hill" and we all would help getting her back on.

Polly had one teacher who had no discipline at all. The kids had no respect for her because they knew they could just get by with anything, and they did. Someone would slip into the schoolhouse and set the clock back. Sometimes they would be out on the playground for an hour when they were only supposed to be out there 15 minutes. Then someone would set the clock back to the right time. It was a bad year. It was Polly's eighth year and all she got out of school was what she had learned the first seven years.

As mentioned before, it was usually high-school girls who had just graduated who taught these schools. These girls were prepared by two years of courses in high school on teaching what was taught in the rural schools. They had an intense six to twelve weeks on the more important subjects like math, English, geography and history. Of course, they got history and English in their regular courses but they studied math intensively. Polly can truthfully say that she learned more math in that 12 weeks of normal training than she did in the ten years she had been in school till then. They also had to take state examinations in each subject. Polly is not sure that she retained it all but it certainly gave her a good strong base for teaching math. There was a manual called the *Course of Study,* that was put out by the state, that was the teacher's bible. It not only outlined what should be taught for each grade but it also gave directions on problems of discipline, public relations, upkeep of the school building, and dealing with children. Polly doesn't think any teacher could have survived without that *Course of Study* and whoever worked on it and created it must have had a very good education and attended a rural school at some time. The rural school kids learned to read and to write. We didn't do a lot of printing but learned to read the print letters. Many of the rural schoolteachers were veterans who had taught rural school many, many years. The girls who went out to teach (and there were a few boys,) had enough enthusiasm and they all needed the jobs badly enough that they put forth their very best effort. None of us have ever regretted going to a rural school, and Polly hopes that she contributed something in the six years that she taught in rural schools.

One of the biggest days in rural schools was May Day. We started the week before the first of May to make May baskets. We used whatever materials we had. If we were lucky enough to get a wallpaper sample book, that made wonderful May baskets. We braided some and we used various boxes that were covered with different kinds of paper and made quite nice little baskets. When May Day came, we and our cousins and either their parents or ours took us to the farthest place away from home with bushel baskets full of May baskets. We didn't have much to put in them but we picked wild flowers and some of us had lilac bushes that were in bloom. We didn't put candy or nuts in the baskets—just flowers because that was all we had or could afford. We went to each place and left a May basket. The idea was to go to the door, leave a basket and run before you were caught. Sometimes, if we thought someone had a really good disposition, we would fix a grab basket. We would hook a long string on it and knock and when someone came to the door we would pull the string and pull the basket out of their reach. We thought this was so funny! Sometimes the man or woman who came to the door laughed just as hard as we did and sometimes they got a little antagonistic. By the time we got the rounds made and got back home, it was night and we were tired. It was something to look forward to and not very exciting to someone who hasn't done it. It seems to us that kids miss out on a lot in not hanging May baskets, especially when they get to the age of admiring a certain girl or boy. What nicer way to show it than to hang them a May basket? Sometimes it nudged a romance along and sometimes it revealed how people felt about each other.

At one school where Polly taught, it was the custom for the men to bring the kids to school when the weather was bad. The men would come in and sit around the fire. While the teacher carried out the ashes, built up the fire, and carried in more fuel, they sat and visited and visited and dripped their muddy shoes on the floor. After they left there was a mess to clean up. That school also had a windmill, which was wonderful. It's the only school that we knew about that had water, but often the pump froze up. These men would sit and talk while the teacher carried the wastepaper basket out and built a fire around the pump to thaw it out. Polly always wondered how they behaved at home because they had no consideration for the teacher. That school and all of the others had outdoor privies and outside coalbins. It was always north of the schoolhouse so that you had to face the wind and it was a cold, heavy, hard job to bring in enough coal to heat those old school buildings. District 9 schoolhouse had a basement and a nice furnace which you could bank at night so it was not quite so freezing in the morning. The fuel was inside next to the furnace, which was great, but we still had the outside privies. It was part of the teacher's job to shovel a path to each privy when it snowed. It wasn't easy and when the teachers nowadays, with all of their conveniences and help, complain about their salaries, Polly often wishes that they could just spend one term in a rural school. Most of the teachers, when Polly was teaching, were working very, very cheaply. Some of them taught for as little as $20/month. Polly always got better wages, although $50/month was the best she ever got. She was very happy to have a job because times were difficult and that money went a long way in those days.

# 4

## *The Country Church*

We had a church in the neighborhood and it had been built, we think, with a lot of praying. It was also fastened together with a lot of praying. It was a poorly built church on top of a hill with no trees to stop the wind and it was very hard to heat. The heat came from a small pot-bellied stove in the middle of the church. The doors opened into a little anteroom and then swinging doors into the church proper. It had a very high ceiling and was quite plain inside. It had wooden pews that were the most uncomfortable things

The Mount Pleasant Church—date unknown

to sit on that you could imagine. Probably, they were built that way so that you would stay awake. We didn't have a regular minister but had itinerant preachers. Occasionally, a man would move into an empty house in the neighborhood and say he was a preacher and then he would preach. Some of them did quite well. One preacher would preach as long as his throat held out. Sometimes it was two hours and sometimes it was three hours. Sometimes he would get through in a hurry. For several years another man and his wife came from another town to preach. They would come every two weeks. He was much loved—a very dear, kind man. Even the kids liked to hear him preach. He preached about how wonderful life was and how much hope we had. His wife was also a minister and very much opposite to him. He was outgoing and cheerful and she was a sour, fearful woman. He preached about living and she preached about dying and it was a sad day when she was going to do the preaching. Usually after church, the minister went home with somebody for Sunday dinner. Another minister came from Sutton, Nebraska. He would come into Inavale on the train and usually someone would meet him. If not, he would walk out to somebody's house and spend the night, have breakfast in the morning and then have church. Then in the afternoon or evening he would leave on the train that went back east. He too was much loved. We don't know if he had a wife since she never came with him. He must have had a wife once because one time he brought a young son with him, who was quite a thrill for the young girls.

We also had church socials. The women had a Ladies Aid Society, which met every couple weeks. They did some sewing and quilting and had a Bible reading. They usually sang some songs and it was more of a social than a religious thing. About once a year, the church would have an ice-cream social. It was usually held in a grove someplace or on a farm that had a stream or a spring that was kind of a cool spot in the summer. Different people would bring freezers of ice cream and cakes. It was advertised and people came from the surrounding areas to be treated to homemade ice cream. Of course, there was a price and the money was used to buy Sunday school supplies. The church, as we said, was poorly built and it was always dusty. Our mother was superintendent for a number of years and she thought it was her job to see that the church was clean for Sunday service. We usually had a hired girl and the Saturday job for Polly and the hired girl was to clean up the church so that it was ready for Sunday morning. Polly always hated to do it because on Saturday afternoon we got ready to go to town on Saturday night. As long as she lived at home and as long as the church was there, that was her job. Very often they worked long and hard to get it cleaned up and a storm would come that night and Sunday morning it would be as bad as ever. That was discouraging and really tested your Christianity.

People came to church in old cars, buggies or farm wagons, and on horseback. One preacher we had always rode a mule. One family had a little Austin car—the only one ever seen in those parts. The wife was very fat and they had removed the front passenger seat so that she could get in. She sat in the back seat and the several children fitted in wherever they could.

We had church there for many years. Finally it was so hard to heat the church and so few people came—sometimes only eight or ten people—that it was hard to continue. One time we went to church and the stovepipe was gone. The stove was two thirds of the way to the back of the church and the stovepipe went all the way to the front of the church and then through the wall and up outside. Probably, somebody just didn't have a stovepipe and that was an easy way to get it. It was surely easier to get it down than it was to put up a new one. Besides, no one had enough money to buy a new one. For one winter, we had church at our house and it was OK. It was sort of an effort to get ready for it and to clean up afterwards. It was muddy and snowy and there was a lot of mud tracked in. Mother felt like it was her duty to keep the church going. Then, for a while, we had permission to have church and Sunday School in the schoolhouse. Eventually, the church folded completely and it was torn down. It was built on Dad's land and he believed that he had deeded the land to the United Brethren church. He wrote to the church to see about buying the land back. They eventually replied that they could find no record of their owning the land so he rearranged the fences and it reverted to pasture. The little cemetery beside the church still exists. Some of the graves are maintained and some are overgrown and neglected.

# 5

## *The Hired Men*

This chapter will be devoted to the male hired help that we had. In general, these people fell into two groups. One was relatively long term, mostly married people, and the other group was composed of single and predominantly transient men. We had two houses used for housing married hired men. During the 1930's, everyone was very poor. Married men were paid $25/month. In addition, they were given a house to live in, a garden spot, a house for raising chickens, and an allotment of milk. Single men were paid $20/month and room and board. There were plenty of takers at this price. Inasmuch as we were fairly big farmers, transients coming into town were often referred to us for employment. In several instances, there were families that came to work for us and for neighboring people. There were Galbraiths that came to work—Ted, for us, and Bill worked for Alf. They stayed for a considerable length of time. There was a family of Smiths that lived in the area—all brothers. There was Bruce, who worked for the Norrises (our aunt and uncle), Walter, who also worked for them for a shorter time, Ransome, who worked for us, and another brother named Lil, who worked off and on, coming and going, and his wife Lily, who was domestic help for us on some occasions. Lil fell out of favor when he got drunk and threatened to beat up our father. Lily had a daughter named Anne Barnes who worked for us as a hired girl for a considerable length of time. Walter Smith's family had a number of children that we remember. One was a dark-haired, dark-eyed beauty named Leona, and there was a younger one named Lucy with whom Allan was in love at about age six.

Then we had a man come whose name was Godfrey. He was a bum and had been riding the rails. He came to work for us—we think to shuck corn. After he had been there for a while, he came to Dad and said he had to quit. Dad asked why and he said that he had "cooties". Dad said he wouldn't turn a dog out with "cooties" and that they would take care of it. Dad went to town and got a whole new set of clothes, underwear and all and some special soap that was probably useless. He took Godfrey down to the basement where we had a hose and a floor drain and had him scrub good with the soap. Dad got rid of all his clothes in the furnace. It was an ongoing battle with "cooties" until he finally left. We don't know of any member of our family having body lice. We do remember several instances of head lice, which usually swept through the school from time to time.

One memorable employee was a man who came in on foot from somewhere unknown. He had a small dirty bag on his back, which he called a suggan. He did not want to sleep in the house and made himself a bed on the ground out east of the house. He worked there for maybe a week or two and then one morning, he did not show up for work. He had left his shoes and his suggan at the spot where he slept and was never seen or heard from again. Dad went through his belongings and found no identifying papers. Everything was infested with lice and, eventually, Dad burned everything.

At one time, we hired two men, one a married man who lived in the tenant house up on the hill and the other a single man who lived in our house. After several months, the married man disappeared, leaving his wife behind. The single man simply moved up on the hill with the wife and they continued their employment for some time.

Food was fairly scarce and was sometimes limited to what they could make with their own hands from their garden and their chickens. On several occasions, the family on the hill would send some of their children down to see if we could spare some grease. We usually had meat fryings from bacon and ham and they would take that and make gravy. We are sure that sometimes grease gravy was their main staple.

Another memorable employee was a man named Bill whose last name we cannot remember. He had a skinny blonde wife who on several occasions disappeared on foot and eventually wound up in town. Bill would finish out his workweek and then go to town and always managed to bring her back home.

One of the longest serving married men was a man named Albert Denton, who was a rather pompous fellow, whom we nicknamed Doodle, after a comic strip character who had "big stuff". We called him that so much among the family that Mom forgot once and referred to him as Doodle when talking to his wife. Mom did some fast talking to explain this and apparently got away with it. The education of all of these employees, both male and female, was very meager. It was unusual to have anybody who had attended high school. In spite of this, the caliber of their work was surprisingly good, to our memory. The men especially were able to use fairly complicated equipment and work a team of four or six horses or mules and do quite well. They also could keep farm machinery and harness in repair.

Harold lived with us for several years. He was a true gentleman. He had had very little help in his lifetime. His father died when he was very young and he had had to quit school to help his mother raise his brothers and sisters. When he came to us in the house, he was very clean and careful and appreciative of anything that came his way. He had grandparents in Inavale four miles away and every weekend he visited with them, usually riding horseback. Sometimes he had other things that he needed to do and Dad gave him the use of our car. He was very good to his grandparents and he always chopped enough wood that they would have enough until he came again. Finally, thinking that they needed help, he hired a young girl who would go in and do cooking, washing and whatever else they needed. Harold eventually married the girl, and after the grandparents died, he moved with her to Colorado. He sometimes came back to see us and we were always happy to see him. He was a good person. He could plant the straightest rows of corn of anyone in the whole neighborhood. The neighbors always laughed that we had him plant the corn next to the road in the direction so that people could see how straight they were. The ones who could not make such straight rows did the planting away from the road.

Of the hired men, the one that Polly remembers best was John. He had spent time in the penitentiary for murder. He came home and found another man in his bed and killed him. She always felt that he should have been rewarded rather than punished. While he was in prison he had learned beadwork. He made rings and various other things. He had also been in a fight and had a terrible scar down one side of his face but, to her, he was one of the kindest men she ever knew. She was ten or eleven and when they played games in the evening, he always said "I'll take the little one for my partner." He made her feel like a princess. He also went to visit his mother every Sunday. It was a long, cold drive in his old Model T car that did not have a top on it. It must have been a most unpleasant trip, but he would leave and come back late at night. He was with us for quite a while. Polly does not know where he went from there but she always felt like he was a real friend.

Most of the farms in the neighborhood were quite small—80 acres or 160 acres at most—and if there were boys in the family, there was not enough work for the father and the boys. The young men or boys sought work from the neighbors since they still liked to live at home. One young farm boy came to work for Dad—we will call him Larry. We don't know how long he was there. He was a fair worker and was clean to have around the house. He had one problem. The house was old and had no bathroom. He decided that the open window would make a good urinal. Mother and Dad realized there were stains down the side of the house (he slept on the second floor) but didn't realize what was going on. Early one morning, Mother happened to walk past the window under his room and heard this cascade of water. Without stopping to think, she went to the window and yelled, "You cut that out!". That was the last of Larry. He didn't even come for breakfast but took off down the road. Probably he was very embarrassed, as well he should have been.

During World War II, it was very difficult to hire farm labor. Many of the men were in the military services and others had gone to work in defense plants for higher wages. We were desperate enough to hire almost anyone in any physical condition. Most of the ones that we could find were exempt from military service for either physical or mental conditions.

# 6

## *The Hired Girls*

The household help, as we recall, were surprisingly good in their ability to cook and do household chores. They had the advantage of being supervised by Polly in many of those difficult years when our mother was disabled. In general, the hired girls were quite good people. It should be explained that working as a hired girl was not considered a degrading situation. The girls ate with the family and in many cases socialized with the family. In some cases girls who did not have to work wanted to work for a woman known as an especially good cook, just to learn from her. One of the problems our mother had was to isolate them from the several male members of the family. There were several occasions in which this got to be a problem and there was at least one occasion where a girl was declared to be redundant because of an affair of this sort.

One of the memorable events in Allan's case was a rather plump and pleasant young woman who came to us when he was maybe seven or eight years old. To give her a room, he was moved from his room into a room with Dick. He got up in the night in his sleep and found his way back to his own room where he entered the young lady's bed and where he woke the next morning. The several hired men who were there at the time quickly learned of this and, of course, made a great deal of fun of it. They all envied him, undoubtedly. He was old enough to understand what they were talking about but not old enough to have entered into any sort of relationship. It was a very embarrassing thing for him at the time.

Most of our food was prepared at home from food that we had grown, preserved or dried ourselves. Polly learned to cook at a very tender age because our mother said she did not like to cook and she taught her as soon as she was old enough and big enough. Polly has loved to cook ever since. All those times that we were growing up we usually had a hired girl and live-in hired men. Some of our hired girls were really characters and some of the hired men were also. One woman who worked for Mother we never did know very well. She used to come occasionally and spend a week with us. She was a lady whom Mother had always treasured both as a friend and hired help. Her name was Mary. The last time that Polly made bread on the farm, Mother said that Mary always beat her bread sponge for five minutes.

Another hired girl we had we will call Handy. She couldn't cook and Mother said she cleaned a room like it was round and ignored all of the corners. However, she had the biggest heart in the world. At that time our mother was quite ill and had a lot of pain. Handy would rub her back and her legs and would always say, "Let me rub you and maybe that will relieve you." But anyway she was a good friend whom we had known all her life and we still call her a friend.

We had lots of high-school girls. They were glad to have work although we did not pay much. The usual pay then was $2 per week and room and board. They had good food and were not overworked. It would have been hard to overwork some of them. Some of them could cook a little and could wash dishes and some could not even do that. One wonders why they were not taught some housekeeping even at 15 or 16 years old.

Then there was Opal. We had had a series of hired girls who were very poor cooks. Mother was not doing very much in the cooking line and Polly was away from home. The bread had been particularly bad for some time. Then Opal came and she could make bread that you would die for. In fact the first week she was there, the bread was eaten almost as fast as she could make it. She made four loaves at a time and for a while she baked bread every day. She was a good fry cook and good help in all ways. Then she was needed at home and we had to look again.

Hazel was next. Hazel came from a good family and was very willing but not very efficient. She was quite enraptured with the minister of her church. She said, "He just walks so Holy!" Hazel left and her sister came to take her place. She was a ball of fire and could do everything that Hazel could not, but school started then and she had to go back to town to school.

Ann worked for us for several years. Her sister lived on a neighboring farm. Ann was probably the best help we ever had. She was very clean and particular, as well as a nice person to have around. She and Polly became good friends. Ann too had been left fatherless at an early age. Her mother did practical nursing and housework so Ann mostly had to live with her brother and sister in their homes, which was not a happy arrangement. They were not very glad to have her since they were living sort of a hand-to-mouth existence also.

One woman came to us one night when Dick was just a baby. She said that she would like to work for us but she didn't like babies and she didn't want to have anything to do with the baby. That was acceptable. She was a good cook and was clean. She hadn't been there two weeks before the baby had made a slave of her. She doted on him just as much as the rest of the family did. She stayed with us for quite a long while, as hired girls went. She finally left to be married. She married a nice man and became a very good mother and a loving aunt, which just goes to show you that a baby's smile goes a long way.

Then we had May who came to us in an almost starving condition. She was so very thin and was a real hardship case. There were several in her family living in very bad conditions. She was not only hungry but she was almost in rags and not very many rags at that. She adapted to our family nicely, soon fattened up, learned our ways and tried very hard to do the things that Mother asked her to do just the way Mother wanted them done. She was with us for quite a while and then met a young man who was a total disaster. She fell in love, married him and had eight children and a very hard life. She always made the best of it, and after the children were in school she did housework around town. He finally died and all of her children turned out very well, all honest, well behaved and none were ever in trouble. She deserves a lot of credit for what she did with her life and what she did with her children's lives.

Mother made delicious burnt-sugar cakes. It seemed like very often the girls who came to work there were hungry since they came from big families and times were hard. One day Mother decided to bake a three-layer burnt-sugar cake. When she went to take the layers out of the pans, one of them crumbled just a little but not enough that it could not be built up as a layer. After a while she got ready to put the cake together and frost it and one layer was gone. She said to the hired girl at the time, "Sarah, where is the other layer of my cake?" Sarah replied, "Well it was kind of crumbled so I et it." Mother had a two-layer cake.

Dick remembers Alberta Seems as his favorite hired girl. She liked to work outside better than inside and she would hurry through her work and then come out to help him with his assignment, including heavy, unpleasant work like cleaning out the chicken coops and spreading gravel.

Some of the girls Mom hired were transients who were just travelling around and came to Red Cloud. If they were running out of money, they would ask around for work and someone would call Mother. She and Dad would go to town and interview the girl. They hired some from local farms also but when things got busy on the farm they were usually needed on their own farms. One girl came and Polly remembers she was the first girl we had ever seen with short hair. They called her Bob because she had bobbed hair. Nobody in Red Cloud that we knew had ever had nerve enough to have her hair cut short. She came to work for us and everybody fell in love with her. Everybody said she was very pretty. She had had a decent life but just wanted to see some more of the world. After a few months she said it was time for her to go on so she left. Another one who came to work for us was a red-headed girl who had a relative in Red Cloud. It wasn't a close relative but there was an old guy who had a junkyard in the south end of Red Cloud who was related and she went to stay with him. She ran around with boys and young men in Red Cloud and built up a kind of colorful reputation. People began to say that she was wild and didn't have very good morals. She needed a job and Mother needed a helper real bad. She called Mother and Mother went into town and talked to her quite a bit. Mother said that she had made a reputation that was not very good since she had been around Red Cloud and she wasn't sure she wanted to hire her if she was going to continue that around her sons. The girl said she knew she had made some mistakes but she was going to reform and promised to walk the straight and narrow. Mother said all right, but she said her two older sons were just a few years apart from her in age and she did not want any friendship between the girl and either of them. The girl said Ok, I won't bother them if they don't bother me. She was an elegant cook. She could cook anything and do it quickly and on time. She was very red-headed and we always called her Red. We don't remember what her name was. She was a lady around our home and she worked there some time, maybe six months or so. She left then and we never heard from her again.

Another girl came then who was born on a farm over in Kansas. She had had a good home and was a good cook who could make wonderful bread and cakes and was easy to get along with. That was about the time that Dick was born. After he was born, he was not a very healthy baby and they had a hard time getting food that he could keep down. She was one of the first to take care of him and if Mother was busy she would always take care of him. Every once in a while her language was a little strange and she would say "He's puking again, get a rag!" She stayed there a long time and finally fell in love with the Norrises' hired man. They lived on the farm next to us. He was a good-looking man who had come there to do corn husking and had stayed on to work by the month. We don't know how it happened—maybe someone put them together—but he would walk down in the evening, less than a half mile. They would talk in the kitchen and sometimes go out for a walk and it got pretty serious. Suddenly though, he just left—just dis-appeared. She had already gotten a ring from him—a cheap ring it turned out—she was really sick about it. She didn't want to stay and work anymore. She wanted to go and do something else.

Then we got another girl and it was much the same story—the Nor-rises' hired man again. They had a wedding date set. She was also a great cook. She had a car and they would go out on dates. She announced that they were going to get married and she was really excited about it. Mother was helping her with wedding plans and helped her with a dress. The date was coming up fast and about a week before the big day he disappeared. She went to bed and stayed in bed most of the time for a week over that. She just couldn't get over it and was sure that something had happened to him. He finally sent her a note and said that he just couldn't go through with it. It didn't help much but at least it ended her worries. It wasn't long after he left that a hired man from a farm about nine miles from us asked her to go out with him and she did. They had a whirlwind engagement and were married within a month after their first date. He was a much better man than the first so she was better off that the first man left her. They were married and had a happy marriage and lived on the same farm where he had worked. He soon became the owner of that farm. He was a good farmer and was a good friend of Alf's. While she worked for us, Alf and Mal would tease her quite a bit. She was always good-natured about it but if it got a little too much she would threaten them. She did the laundry and would say, "If you don't cut that out, I'm going to starch your underwear." As far as we know, they are still living on that same farm.

# 7

## *The Mules*

**D**ad always farmed with mules. Alf, who farmed part of the farm, used horses and bred half of his mares with a jackass to produce mule colts for Dad. When old enough these young mules were then broken to harness. The other half of his mares he bred with stallions to replenish his stock of horses. Mules have several advantages over horses when used as horsepower. For example, doing heavy work in high heat, a horse may work until it dies. A mule will almost always stop before that point and refuse to do any more until it has rested and cooled off. Also, a horse will get into rich food and eat until he founders while a mule will eat as much as he can handle and then quit. One might think from this that mules are smarter than horses, which is true. They are also more stubborn (hence the term mule-headed), lazier and generally more difficult to handle. Dad usually had about six or eight trained mules and two or three young mules, which were more or less broken to harness and could be used selectively, usually harnessed with one or more older mules.

Dick was home alone one day and kept hearing an intermittent banging noise. When he finally investigated, he found that the truck that had delivered a load of oats that morning had clipped the barn and split a board. A mule had found that if he hammered on the board with his hoof, he got a little trickle of oats out. He would hammer until he had a little pile of oats and then stop to eat them. Dick got a hammer and nails and fixed the crack. He watched and the mule never bothered to try it again when he saw it was fixed.

Dobbin, one of the mules, was quite musical. If you were walking down the road with a wagon and whistling, Dobbin would swing his big ears back and forth in time with the music, much like a conductor directing an orchestra. If you stopped whistling, both ears would swivel back pointing at you to see what was wrong! Dobbin was also particularly lazy. He would ease back until his end of the doubletree was resting against the wagon and the other mule was doing all of the pulling.

Dick liked to ride the mules even though their bony spines were not very comfortable riding bareback. One time he was riding down to play with another boy who lived several miles away. He was on a young mule that he had never ridden before and was a little nervous about it. When he was almost at the friend's house, he noticed a huge fly had landed on the mule's neck. For fear that this might spook the young mule, he leaned down and slapped the fly. At this the mule stopped dead, put his head down, and Dick somersaulted over his head onto the road. He picked himself up and found the mule standing 20 feet away facing towards home. He walked toward the mule and the mule walked toward home. He ran after the mule and the mule broke into a trot. Dick slowed up and the mule slowed up. Dick was stuck with the humiliation of following 20 feet behind the mule. However, he had a plan. Halfway home, the road made a right angle bend for half a mile, so, when they approached that point, Dick cut across the bend to head off the mule. Unfortunately, the mule also had a plan and broke into a trot. When Dick reached the road again, the mule was standing waiting for him and they continued home—Dick again 20 feet behind the mule.

When the mules were brought in from the pasture to the barn, they knew which stall they were supposed to go into. You prepared in advance by putting their oats into the box in their stall so they were eager to get into the stall. For each mule, there was a halter already attached by a short rope to the front of the stall. The idea was that while they were eating the oats, you would walk in beside them and slip the halter over their head. Some of them had the annoying habit of waiting until you picked up the halter and then backing up until the rope would not quite reach so you could put on the halter. If you went out to drive them up, they would quickly start eating the oats again. They obviously thought this was fun since they would do it over and over again. The only solution was to go out and lambaste them on the rear with a broken tug kept for that purpose to convince them that the game was not worth it. Sometimes, you wondered if the mules were not smarter than you were.

Dick seemed to have special problems with the mules, partly because he was small for his age. In order to harness the mules, he had to stand up on one of the boards forming the side of the stall to get the harness over the mule's back. One day he was harnessing Pete, who was busily eating his oats. As he threw the harness over Pete's back, Pete leaned over, pinching him against the stall side. This straightened him up and his feet left the board he was standing on and there he was with his feet dangling in midair. He was too small to push the mule over and Pete ignored his yells and pounding on his back with his fists. Dick tried jerking up his knees into the mule's belly but beyond a gentle whoosh this had no effect. After five minutes or so, Pete finished his oats and decided to release him. If mules can smirk, he was smirking.

During World War II, the army had a demand for mules to be used in mountainous countries where wheeled vehicles could not penetrate. The mules could carry large pack loads and could handle almost any terrain that people could. This was especially true in the Italian campaign. We had army buyers come through the area periodically looking for mules and we sold several to them. A curious fact was that the army would buy any color mule but it had to be "mealy-mouthed", that is, have a whitish nose. Mules are mostly brown but can be red, white or almost any color that a horse can be. Mealy mouths are common but not universal and we never could see that mealy-mouthed mules were any better than others.

# 8

## *Health Conditions*

The physicians in those early days had a hard life. Often they had to drive ten miles or more in a team and buggy to visit a sick patient or deliver a child. Sometimes, the weather was miserable—rain, snow, sleet—and the roads were barely improved. A doctor might spend all night with a patient and then get a call that he was needed on another farm. He frequently ate meals at the patient's house. Dad asked Dr. Packwood once if he ever found himself in a house that was so dirty that he did not want to eat there. He replied that in that case he just told them he had to leave and please hard-boil him a couple eggs to take with him. The advent of automobiles did not help that much because of the miserable condition of the roads. With the buggy, once he started home, the doctor could go to sleep and rely on the horses to find their way home. Often when we called a doctor after the advent of automobiles, we would be told that the roads were so bad he could not get there. In that case, we would meet him at the highway with a team and wagon and ferry him back and forth over the country roads.

We were told of a case where a neighbor had a sick child. Mom had been called in to help. She told Dad that she did not think the baby would live if they could not get a doctor. The roads were drifted with snow and Dad did not think he could get to town but he tried. When he came to a drift, he would back up and ram into it with his Model T Ford until he broke through. Of course, he killed the engine frequently. The Model T had the crank permanently mounted in the front and finally he bent it to the point that he could not turn it to restart the car. He managed to tear a fence post out beside the road and

57

used it as a lever to bend the crank out again. He actually managed to get to town and bring back a doctor but the baby died that night anyway.

The cost of medicine then was considerably different than today. There was no insurance and there was quite a restriction on the number of procedures that could be performed on a patient. The price of an office visit in the early 1930's was somewhere from 50 cents up to a dollar or two. The price of a prescription usually ran less than a dollar. Office visits and house calls were often paid for in commodities, and it was not uncommon to receive such things as chickens and produce in return for medical care. In spite of this, physicians were probably one of the groups that did best financially in the days of the deep depression.

It is to be noted that the physicians of that time were very poorly prepared in comparison with those of today. Many of them had not attended medical school but had received their degrees by preceptorship. Our personal physician during our later years was Dr. Obert and it was known that he was in truth a graduate of the University of Kansas. He was considered to be in advance of the knowledge at that time. We do not know about the educational backgrounds of earlier family physicians, such as Dr. Packwood. The armamentarium at that time was very meager, to say the least. There were very few medicines known to them that are known to us today. There were no antibiotics until after World War II. We had sulfonamides in the late 1930's. At the early onset of WWII, our father tore away a large flap of skin from the back of his hand in a washing machine wringer and he was seen by a doctor who treated the wound by packing it full of sulfonamide powder. He developed an allergy to the powder and got a rash, which ascended his forearm. He again consulted medical care and was told he had erysipelas and was given sulfonamides by mouth. He later necrotized the entire flap and spent several months recovering from this wound.

A neighbor girl married a man from Arkansas, who was of very limited mental capacity and they came to live in one of our tenant houses. She became pregnant and delivered prematurely. Our mother officiated at that delivery and the baby was an anencephalic fetus. It was not viable and it was born, died, and buried, probably without any medical reporting. Alf made a tombstone out of concrete and Clarence Fitz made a casket out of wood from the organ in the old church, which two of us had mostly disassembled for the reeds. The casket was lined with Polly's white graduation dress. On a recent visit to the cemetery, it was noticed that someone has placed a nice commercial tombstone on the grave. We were pleased to see that the old concrete tombstone is still in place.

Because of the shortcomings of formal medicine, people developed various techniques to take care of their own problems. Our mother developed a number of skills over the years, which were more or less self-taught. In the Mexican culture, she would have been known as a curandera and was often the first one consulted in times of injury or sickness. She had developed methods of treatment of various wounds. Lacerations were treated by proper cleansing with soap and water, which is good even by today's standards. There were no ways of taping wounds shut as there are today and she had no techniques for suturing of wounds. Her treatment after cleansing consisted of applying various ointments. She had invented and sewn together various dressings, which fitted fingers and toes, which she called fingerstalls and toestalls. She understood the principles of infection and had a system of disinfecting skin and wounds with mercuric chloride. We remember clearly the bottle was labeled with a skull and crossbones, and we were reminded frequently never to have any contact with this medication. Painkillers consisted mainly of aspirin and also we had a proprietary mixture from a travelling route salesman. It was called Baker's Pain Reliever, which was primarily a mixture of alcohol and sodium salicylate. It was effective, but it was very nasty and we tried to avoid it at all cost. She had a system of making poultices. She believed that infection could be drawn away from the body with the proper mixture of poultices. She had devised several mixtures for treating boils and carbuncles. One of her favorites was a mixture of soap and sugar. Another was cooking flaxseed into a gelatinous mass, which she then applied over a boil. She knew enough that when a boil had gathered or come to a head, she could lance it with a needle sterilized in mercuric chloride. The core could be removed and that would usually cure the problem. At one point in our family we had a small epidemic of skin infections—pimples, boils and carbuncles—and our brother Alf had a serious problem over a long period of time with repeated infections. Laxatives were felt to be a great part in the treatment of disease and our father especially felt that most problems could be cured by purging the body with various laxatives. Castor oil was the most potent and the most dreaded and we were sometimes paid to take castor oil. Other laxatives included Pluto Water, which was a mineral water, and Inner Clean, which is still being manufactured to this day. We dreaded these so much that if we had any problems we would always report that we had diarrhea so we would not be subjected to these laxatives.

Our mother had a special interest in obstetrics and acted as sort of the neighborhood midwife. There was no hospital so all babies were delivered at home. Sometimes a doctor could not get there because of road conditions and sometimes people could not afford a doctor. She always kept a box of white rags that had been washed, then ironed thoroughly, and put away in newspapers. Polly thought this was strange, but a Red Cross nurse told her that the news print kept things fairly sterile. She always kept ready a kerosene lamp, a package of safety pins, extra newspapers that were put away, folded and clean, and the box of rags. She had developed a technique of hot packing the perineum to prepare it for the extrusion of the baby's head. If someone came to the door in the middle of the night with a request to come and help his wife have a baby, she would gather up the things that she had ready and go. She would come home when the baby had been delivered. In most cases there were other neighbor ladies there as well as the family. If the doctor got there in time it was fine but if he did not, the babies seemed to come into the world just the same. Mother had a textbook of female health problems, *The Wholesome Woman,* which she studied intensively and she was a source of advice for all sorts of female complaints, obstetric and otherwise.

Local anesthesia was unknown before WWII. If pain relief was necessary for fractures or treatment of wounds, it was accomplished by open-drop ether. Dick lacerated his lower leg on one occasion and they took him to Riverton to see a Dr. Packwood. A dentist associated with Dr. Packwood administered drop ether to suture the laceration, after which he returned home. Fractures were often treated without anesthesia, and Mal at one time had a displaced fracture of his forearm reduced without anesthesia. Often the patient would faint during the procedure and thus limit the pain to some degree. One day a neighbor, Bruce Smith, was cutting down a tree, which fell on him and fractured a forearm and trapped him under the tree. Alf and Allan were called to come and get him loose and he was in such pain that they had to get a doctor to come and give him some relief before they could saw off the branch and release him. A Dr. Bowles, a D.O., came with an assistant, who was not a professional person, and she delivered open-drop ether there in the feedlot while they sawed the branch off.The doctor reduced the fracture and strapped a yucca board on it. There were no casts available at that time, and yucca boards and bandages were the main means of immobilization of fractures. To our knowledge there were no means of x-rays in that area until about WWII.

It is noted that there was no formal workmen's compensation during that time. The last state Workmen's Compensation Act was enacted in 1948, and that exempted domestic and farm workers from coverage. Farm work is dangerous work, and it is surprising that we did not have more serious injuries. The only really bad one was to a married man who worked for Alf, and had one weak leg from childhood polio. He consistently wore overalls that were too long and dragged on the ground. One day he got the dangling overalls caught in the power take-off on the tractor and it tore off the weak leg. He was never able to adapt to an artificial leg and eventually killed himself. There were other injuries in the neighborhood, such as hands caught in chain drives and injuries in runaways. One gruesome story was of a neighbor who managed to bale himself up in a bale of hay.

Smaller problems revolved around various transmissible diseases. At one time in our family we developed an epidemic of streptococcosis. Several of us had scarlet fever and Mal and Allan developed glomerulo-nephritis (kidney infection). They were treated with bed rest for a number of months. Allan remembers putting his cherry-colored urine in the window each day and Mother would take a reading and phone it in to Dr. Packwood in Riverton, who would advise her on further treatment, of which there was actually none. During this time, we had to have our house posted for quarantine, and at the end of this period we had to fumigate all of our books and bedding and all of the rooms in which we had been treated. Other diseases that required quarantine were measles, chicken pox and whooping cough. Whooping cough was a particularly dreaded disease. At one point, Dick, as an infant, developed whooping cough and was extremely ill for nearly a year. It was difficult for him to take food without vomiting during his coughing episodes and his physical development was very slow during that time. The prime nutritional supplement for him during that time was dextromaltose. Parasites were quite common, especially as new people moved into the community and brought in new problems. Almost every year at our little country school there would be an epidemic of scabies, which we called the itch. Invariably, when one got it, everyone would get it. It was treated with a mixture of lard and sulphur. Head lice were fairly common and several episodes of this occurred during our years at District 9 school. These were treated with various techniques, one of which, was a proprietary product called Blue Ointment, which was a mercuric chloride preparation.

There were other cases of major illnesses. One concerned the Hummel family. They apparently had typhoid fever one summer and, as best we can remember, the father and mother and three or four children died, leaving one child alive. They occupy a plot in the Mt. Pleasant cemetery, with all of the graves surrounded by an iron fence. The other event occurred when the Walt Shelton family got what was reported to be typhoid fever. There is some doubt about this diagnosis, but at any rate the whole family was sick all summer. It was a very hot summer and they were camped out in a tent-like situation. The neighbors all brought food and support for them. It was said at the time that it had come from a contaminated well. In making these diagnoses, it should be noted that there was no such thing as bacteriology in those parts at that time. There was another episode in which there were several cases said to be smallpox. It was quite a scare at the time. We were all taken into town and vaccinated by a Dr. Stockman. There was such a demand for vaccine that there was not enough to go around, and several of us were vaccinated with material from under the scabs of people who already had active vaccinations. Due to the fact that all of the people who supposedly got the disease lived, it is doubtful that this was smallpox but more likely a severe case of chickenpox. At one time we had a scare in the neighborhood that there was a case of diphtheria, and the school district paid to have the whole school inoculated. Even though this was an area, which was agricultural, and agricultural workers were frequently wounded, and there was no tetanus immunization, we do not know of any case of tetanus during this time. The children were all predominantly barefooted during the summer, not only for their preference, but because many of them had no shoes. Puncture wounds of the feet were frequent, and it should have been a fertile time for tetanus if there ever was one,

Animal related injuries were quite common either from horses and mules while working them or from other animals while taking care of them. At one point, our father was dragged by a team of mules and received extensive chest injuries, which were diagnosed as rib fractures without the benefit of x-rays. Dick had a runaway with a team of mules while operating a hay rake. He was thrown under the rake and had a rake tooth driven through the calf of his leg.

One memorable injury at school was an accident to a boy named Junior Stratton. He fell off a monkey bar, striking his head and rendering him totally unconscious. He was taken to his home and did not regain consciousness for several months. During that time, he was sustained to some degree with rectal administrations with glucose water made from corn syrup. He must have had a cerebral hemorrhage but since there was no hospital and no way of diagnosing or treating, there was not all that much made of the whole thing. He did recover fully.

One major health problem arose when Dick, as a preschool child, drank kerosene from a tin can. We drank several things from tin cans at that time and it seemed natural to him to drink it. At the time, we all thought he was going to die. Dr. Packwood was consulted and he came from Riverton and pumped the stomach with a long catheter. Today that would be considered a very improper treatment. At any rate, he survived. On one occasion, Allan became quite ill from a bilateral ear infection, which finally ruptured on both sides. He was treated with a hot-water bottle and Dad blowing cigarette smoke in his ears, and Dr. Packwood provided codeine pills, which was considered quite romantic treatment at that time.

Mom had some of these codeine pills left over and she hoarded these jealously for treatment of some of our most dire problems. She also had acetanilide in her armamentarium but she was very fearful of this drug and we do not remember her ever using it. The remainder of her pharmacy consisted of various nostrums from the peddlers, such as Raleigh salesmen and the Baker people, who came around selling drugs, tea, coffee, spices, etc. She had several cough medicines, an enzyme medicine called Takadiastase which was good for anything in the realm of the abdomen, and, when all else failed, various tonics such as cod liver oil. There was no knowledge of vitamins at that time. One of the most dreaded tonics was called Elixer of I Q & S, iron, quinine and strychnine sulfate. It was one of the most horrid-tasting mixtures ever and we fought it at all costs.

During the late 1930's, our mother's health deteriorated because of tuberculosis of the spine. Because of the absence of x-rays, the diagnosis was not made and she was diagnosed and mis-diagnosed for a number of things and treated with various modalities, which became a desperate search for some help. During this time, she was away from home quite a bit and quite indisposed and her mothering capabilities suffered. These duties were transposed onto Polly, who became sort of mother in charge at the time. There were several hired girls during this period who were quite good at mothering and they also helped fill in for the absent mother during these times. Mom was treated with a number of things, including at one time chiropractic, which left her partially paralyzed. This was one of the things that finally brought the thing to a real crossroads. At one time too, she had all of her teeth removed because of the possibility that they might be poisoning her system and causing this disease. Finally, the problem was made clear at the Mayo Clinic, which was then in its fairly early days and was receiving good reports throughout the Midwest. She was treated with a bone graft from the tibia to fuse the diseased spine. A Dr. Ghormley treated her there, and, in later years, his nephew became a partner of Allan's.

In the late 1940's, our mother began to feel ill again and underwent investigation in several places. Allan was in medical school at the time and he brought her to his school where he had her examined by some of his supervisory staff. At that time she was having low-grade fever and several other abnormal lab tests were taken, not finding the site of the problem. Several years later, while Allan was stationed in Germany, she made plans to come and visit. However, she developed what was known as a cold abscess in her groin, which was an extension of a tuberculous abscess from her old spinal tuberculosis, which had lain dormant during that time. By this time, they had new and better drugs to treat tuberculosis and she was apparently successful in conquering this problem and never did have any more trouble from it. The exact cause of her infection was never determined and none of the rest of the family ever suffered from this disease. It is probable that she contracted this disease from either the ingestion of raw milk or tuberculous meat. This could have happened in childhood and lain dormant for many years before it became apparent. There was no such thing as pasteurization of milk in those pre-war years. There were, however, several sporadic attempts of the government to come to the farm and skin test our milk cows for tuberculosis. None were ever found to be infected. Refrigeration of milk products was very inadequate in those days, compared to modern standards. Our milk was all separated and the cream was used for making butter. The cream was not refrigerated but kept at basement temperature and not until after churning was the butter ever refrigerated.

Allan's birth certificate lists his birth weight as 12 pounds! While helping her with a long ago problem, he had occasion to review Mom's x-rays. It occurred to him that it would be quite difficult to get a 12-pound fetus through that pelvis. We were all birthed at home. He asked her, "How was my weight determined at birth?" She said that after the delivery she asked the doctor the birth weight. "What do you want him to weigh?" he answered. She said, "My husband said if I gave him a 12-pound boy he would take me to Kansas City." "That's what he weighed," was the answer. Makes sense. The only scale we remember was a brass, hand-held thing with a hook, probably not much better than her method.

In our neighborhood, there was a woman who took care of her family for years and then moved into Red Cloud. She took women into her home who were waiting to deliver, about two at a time. She worked closely with the doctors and was a practical nurse herself. She had many babies delivered in her home and she loved every one of them. She kept track of "her babies" as long as she lived. The women got tender, loving care, delicious food and comfortable surroundings. Other women would start little home nurseries. There were several practical nurses who could help out in sickness. There was one lady, who was always called Maw, who was delightful. If we had any serious illness in our family, we always called for Maw to come and stay a few days. That was about the best medical care we could get unless we went to Hastings, which was 40 miles from Red Cloud over a graveled road.

When a person died, the neighbor ladies always went in to help lay out the body. The body was usually kept at home, and somebody sat up with it until time for the funeral. That was partly respect and partly, we have been told, because the houses were not screened, and animals were attracted by the smell of death and would often try to get into the house. That may be an old wives' tale, but it is one that we have heard many times.

Both our mother and our father recognized the benefit of nutrition in the prevention of disease. We were very fortunate in that despite the extreme poverty conditions of the depression and the dust bowl, we always had proper foods. We raised the bulk of our own food, both animal and vegetable, and our parents emphasized the value of a diversified diet in the prevention of disease and the maintenance of health. This was not true for many of the families at that time.

School lunches were in general quite good for our family, but there were children who brought pitifully poor lunches. Sometimes we shared or swapped lunches but there were some children that could not swap lunches because of the very poor quality of their food. This was a very sad thing and we don't know how in the world we stood it at the time. There was a family of sharecroppers named Jorgensen who were extremely poor. They came in at a time when there were no crops and they had no income. There was at that time a system for providing such people with what were called commodities, which were giveaway items, such as flour, sugar and lard. This family had a number of children and we remember them coming to school with their lunches. They would make very poor bread with the flour, a dark, hard bread, and they would put lard on it and salt and pepper. They called it salt-and-pepper bread and this was all the food that they brought to school for weeks at a time. We are sure that various vitamin deficiencies must have been rampant although we did not know about them at the time. One day, Allan had a banana in his lunch, which was quite an extraordinary event. One of these kids saw him eating it and asked if it melted in his mouth, because he had never had a banana. Allan wonders now how he had the guts to eat that banana without sharing it with him. On another day, an older boy, Leonard Griffiths, came to school with an orange. This was considered a very outstanding event. When someone came to school with an orange, kids would stand around and ask for peelsies, which were considered a delicacy at that time. On this occasion, Leonard peeled the orange and it was a blood orange. No one had ever seen or heard of such a thing, and the teacher announced that it was spoiled, and it was thrown away.

Several times a winter when Polly was teaching at District 9, we would make a stew or potato soup. We had a kettle in our school, and on those occasions children would bring things to put in the pot—maybe a carrot or a potato or some milk. On one occasion, a new child in the district brought goat's milk, and that was considered very unusual. At any rate, we made very good hobo stew in the pot, and those were days that everybody had a good lunch.

# 9

## *Economic Conditions*

A few of the larger farm owners employed married hired men and furnished them a house for their families to live in. They were able to have a rent-free place to live and if they wanted to get out and do it they could cut wood to warm the house. They were usually allowed a supply of milk and a low wage. Of course, at that time all wages were low. There were many families who lived in very crowded quarters. We know of one family that lived in a six-room house with another family, and each family had six children. Each family had three rooms and it must have been very crowded and not very sanitary. It is hard to see how they got along, but the two men were brothers and that may have helped. Their existence was more hand-to-mouth than you could call a good living, but they were uneducated and were really incapable of doing anything other than farm work. It was not as difficult to be a farmer then as it is now. On our farm we had men who stayed for several years and some who moved in and out almost overnight. The poor wives were very much overworked; they had to manage with not very much money and no medical care to speak of. There was no welfare or help other than what the family could provide. Families helped each other. One family that we can remember drove into our farm one evening and the children were out playing around. They said that they had taken the baby to the doctor that day. Mother asked what the problem was and was told that the doctor didn't know for sure but he thought the baby might have diphtheria. At that time, diphtheria was one of the most dreaded diseases. Immediately, Mother rounded up us kids and got us into the house. The diagnosis must have been wrong since there were no deaths, and we heard no more about it.

That was a time when the neighbors traded work. It was a big deal because the wheat had to be cut and shocked and dried, and the thrashing crew came in later. It meant as many as 12 to 14 men for dinner (this was the noon meal; at night we had supper). Sometimes we had most of them for supper, also. When there were so many men to feed, it took lots of food. It always happened that there were some good places to eat and some bad, and at the bad places, most of the men always had something to do at home so they could not stay to eat. It seemed like at our house they always stayed for dinner and supper both. Polly can remember getting up in the morning and dressing four or five chickens and making four or five pies and baking bread. It was a big day and a hard day. The men worked hard and it was hot. The chaff from the wheat or other small grains was very irritating to the skin and to the nose. Our brother Alf had a thrashing machine and he had a knack, it seemed, at a place where the food wasn't good, of having the machine always break down so he would have to go to town to get repairs. The other people got to stay and have dinner. He had lots of stories to tell about different places where he worked and lots of praise for some of them.

South of us there were five or six small farms—80 acres or so. Usually there was a mother and father and several children. They were apt to marry within the neighborhood. In fact there was no place else to go. Most of them had finished no more than the eighth grade in school and had no trade except farming. Eighty acres with horses or mules was not a full-time job and not much of a living.

Much of the trading, buying and selling that was done in the neighborhood was bartering. People didn't have any money but they traded commodities that they had in abundance and they traded themselves. If a farmer needed extra help, the neighbors came and worked and got a day's work in return in the future but no money changed hands. If one person had a lot of sweet corn and another had watermelons, they swapped back and forth so everybody had some. There were people we called "medicine men", who went through the country from farm to farm. The Raleigh man and the Baker's man and the KKK man went from door to door selling spices and patent medicines and many things that you needed. The Raleigh man's vanilla was especially good and there are people yet who try to find a Raleigh store that has vanilla. If you didn't have money to buy something, these peddlers would take a chicken or a dozen eggs, a watermelon or whatever you had that you could spare, and again no money changed hands. Also, some women would hang wallpaper together. If someone's house needed to be papered, they would get together and do the papering. They all seemed to be talented in hanging wallpaper, which is almost a lost art anymore. Then when the next lady needed wallpaper they would all get together again and do it. There was no such thing as babysitters in those days. If you had children and you could not take care of them for an hour or two, or a day or a week, you traded with relatives or neighbors. Sometimes, you traded kids just so the kids got a change and saw a different way of living. Also, going door to door, were people selling vacuum cleaners, although few people had the money to buy one or had the electricity to run one. There were also people selling magazine subscriptions. *Capper's Weekly* seemed to be especially anxious to sell subscriptions. They would take an old hen or a rooster for a year's subscription. In many homes, it was the only newspaper that they took. When we had current events at school, half the kids would have the same current event because they took it from the *Capper's Weekly*. It is still published after all these years.

Another job where work was traded, and still is, is that of working their cattle, bringing them in from the pasture and marking them, castrating them and picking those to get ready to sell. There were usually four or five men who worked together and did the cattle at one place one day and another place the next. They were mostly untrained people but they had learned from experience and usually had pretty good luck. In dire cases, they would call the veterinary. In most cases the farmers would know what to do as well as the veterinary. They still do some of this, since they do not like to spend the money to have the veterinary come out to the farm and do it.

There were many people who came into the neighborhood and moved out the next year. There were people who were very, very poor. There were people who came into the school who were actually hungry, but as we look back at some of the pictures of the Sunday school and the school, the children looked well cared for. Their overalls were old but they were patched, not ragged, and they always looked clean. Their mothers were overworked. They had to do the washing with a washboard and the ironing with sad irons heated on the kitchen stove. Most of the mothers did remarkably well.

One thing that brought the neighbor ladies together was the fact that chicken feed was put up in cloth sacks of rather coarse material but beautiful prints. A large sack of chicken feed would make an apron. Two and a half sacks would make a dress. Money was pretty scarce and the material cut down the price of the chicken feed. Ladies were very careful about opening the bags, which were sewn shut with a chain stitch. They washed the sacks carefully and ironed them and when some of the ladies got together they took their feed sacks with them hoping that they could match two or three alike. If you only had one sack, you could make excellent dishtowels. It was sort of a contest as to who could make the prettiest dress out of feed sacks. The white sacks were made into pillowcases. We slept on many a feed-sack, sugar-sack or flour-sack pillowcase. Polly wore many pairs of underpants that were made out of flour sacks and she had one pair that said Mother's Best across the seat. It was hard to get the ink out of the labels and after they started making printed ones, they used paper labels, which was a blessing because there were a lot of nice things that people were able to make out of them. They made quilts and used pieces to reinforce worn clothes and blankets. It was a time of do without, make do or do over and we learned a lot of things in the '30's that we still practice. We are thankful that we had a mother and father who taught our family to make the best of what we had.

The people in our neighborhood were always helpful in time of trouble or death. You could always count on the neighbors pitching in, which may be a habit of Midwesterners. If there was a farmer who was ill at planting time, the neighbors would help get the crop in. Or at harvest time in the fall, if the farmer was disabled or had serious trouble in the family, they had a husking bee or a get-together to get in the crop. In later years there were combines and corn pickers, and farmers were generous in bringing in their equipment and men to help out. That meant lots of cooking for the women, who also pitched in and brought all kinds of cooking imaginable. At the time of a death in the family or serious trouble, the food came pouring in. Everybody in the neighborhood brought cakes, pies, salads, desserts and casseroles and you were just overwhelmed with wonderful food. Unless you have experienced it, you cannot realize what a blessing it was.

There were times when people were terribly needy and they would have a shower for a new baby or a new bride and groom. People in the 1930's didn't have very much but they shared generously what they had. At Christmas time, if there was a minister in the community or a teacher who was struggling, people would have a pound party where you would bring a pound of anything. There was a pound party for a minister in town once, and they had hams and turkeys and roasts and all kinds of canned foods. They had a little boy who looked at the table and said, "There isn't a bit of candy in that whole thing." That was tragic to him, but probably not to his parents.

One of the most important things on the farm was the telephone. At best, it barely worked. Not everybody had a telephone. The lines were a joke. Often there were no insulators. Some of the lines were nailed to a fence post and sometimes there was a 2x4 stuck in the ground for a post. If a farmer came along and saw the line was down he would be apt to nail it to a tree. We had a party line. There were five to ten people on each party line. Each person had a number and ours was 3 on

24. You called the operator by cranking a long ring on your telephone and when she answered you would ask for 3 on 24. The three meant that the operator would connect you to the 24 line and give two long rings. Usually, when you picked up your receiver, everyone else on the line picked theirs up also so they could listen. Since each phone weakened the signal, that made it that much harder to hear. This practice was known as "rubbering". Rubbering was especially interesting if a young girl or man on the line was courting. If he or she got a call from a new person, this was even more interesting and as soon as they hung up, the neighbors would start calling each other to talk about it. If you gave out a recipe on the telephone, before the week was out everyone on the line had tried that recipe. One woman said that she had tried the recipe but it didn't turn out very well. She couldn't hear very well and couldn't tell whom to call to get the right measures.

Sometimes if we were calling Mom and she couldn't hear us, one of the rubberers would speak up and tell her what we were trying to say.

If you needed a doctor, you either went to a neighbor who had a telephone or went to town to get him. Our family doctor for many years, Dr. Packwood, lived in Riverton, a very small town six miles west of Inavale. He was a very big man and very profane but also very kind. He probably did not have a great deal of education but he had a lot of common sense and experience and was always willing to come day or night and stay as long as he was needed. One time one of our brothers was very sick and they didn't think he was going to live. We finally got a message through to our doctor. Roads were very bad and he said he could only get as far as Inavale but if someone could meet him there with a team of mules and wagon, he would come. The roads were so bad that by the time the hired man got home with the doctor, the team was too exhausted to take him back the next morning and we had to bring in a new team.

In the late 1930's and early 1940's, grasshoppers were a major plague. At times, they would arrive in such numbers that they would eat a developing corn crop down to the ground and even down into the ground in a few days. A hammer or axe left out in the field would have the surface of the handle eaten off, as they were apparently attracted by the salt from sweaty hands. Their only virtue was that they made good fish bait. We would go out with a wet gunnysack to catch them. You could slap a small weed with the gunnysack and stun a dozen or more with one swat. They seemed to stay alive on the hook for some time and their struggles attracted the fish. The government provided help through the county agricultural agents in the form of poison bait and spreaders. The bait was sawdust mixed with arsenic and molasses. The spreader was an oil drum on wheels with a wheel-driven propeller underneath to scatter the bait as it was towed along. We do not recall any particular precautions taken in handling the bait. It would certainly be considered quite unsafe today.

Another pest of those days was the prairie dog. They would form towns where half or more of the grass was either eaten or covered up with dirt from their burrows. They were also a hazard to horses when you were rounding up cattle from a pasture infested with them. Their holes were nicely sized to break a horse's leg. Dick's first paying job, at about the age of 11, was poisoning prairie dogs on Uncle Lawrence's pasture about a mile away. He would ride over there on our cow pony, with a gallon glass jug full of carbon disulfide. The technique would be to have a shovel, a tin can, the jug of carbon disulfide, and a sack of corncobs. Corncobs were soaked in carbon disulfide in the tin can and dropped down each prairie dog hole and then a shovelful of dirt was placed over the hole. With weekly treatments over the course of a summer, he was able to eliminate the prairie dog town. Nowadays, this would be considered too hazardous for an adult, let alone a kid. In addition, prairie dogs are protected at least in some areas. They were great fun to try to shoot with a .22 rifle. You would often spend 15 minutes or more sneaking up close enough to shoot and then one would spot you and give a warning whistle with every dog disappearing before you ever got a shot.

During the drought, we often had dust storms. These could come up quite suddenly and visibility was almost zero. It was said that some of this dust had come from as far away as Oklahoma. One evening one came up just before supper and although our house was relatively new and tight, a lot of dust was coming into the house. Mom covered all of the food and put it in the cupboard and we waited until it was over to eat supper. Our house had a screened porch on two sides and after such a storm, the men would have to come in with scoop shovels and shovel out most of the dust before Mom and the smaller kids could sweep out the rest.

This was a time when airplanes were just beginning to appear. In the earliest days we never saw any airplanes but after WWI we occasionally saw one of the WWI Jennys. We only saw one every two or three months and everyone would run outside shouting "airplane" if we heard one. About 1930 or '31 an air circus came to Red Cloud and put on a show. They had wing walkers and parachute jumps and planes doing stunts, as well as planes that would take passengers for rides. Mal was there with a high school friend, and they were offered a ride on a five-passenger plane for something like $2. They took them up and just flew around for a few minutes. It was pretty exciting since they had never been up before but in the end pretty tame. There was another plane there that had been doing stunts so they went and asked the pilot for a ride in it. It would only take two people and Mal thinks they had to pay $5 each for that, which was all the money they had. The pilot took them up and they said they would like to have some acrobatics, and he obliged. It was really fun and they enjoyed the rest of the show. There was a girl in Red Cloud who had met one of the guys in the show and gone out with him. Before the three days were over, she was up riding with him all the time. When the show left, she went too. Everyone wondered what would happen to her. We heard after a while that she had become a parachute jumper. She would jump out of a plane one or more times every day. We then heard that she had married this guy, but she went on with the parachute jumping. She won some prizes for being the first woman to jump from so many thousand feet or falling so far before opening her parachute. That was quite an exciting thing for Red Cloud to have a girl in an air circus. Last we heard she had stayed in the parachute jumping business and had become a pilot also.

In Hastings about 1930 or '31, probably after the air circus went through, there was a guy who decided to build an airplane. He had worked on it for a couple years. We don't know anything about his history. At the same time there was a guy in Hastings who had started an airplane school teaching people to fly. One of our neighbors, Harold Rudd, was a little older than Mal and was a friend of his, and Harold decided to learn to fly. He went up to Hastings for several weeks and learned to fly. He loved it and they hired him to stay there and be a teacher. There were a couple more from Inavale that learned to fly there and one of them was looking for a job but jobs flying were pretty scarce. The guy who was making the plane, which he named *Maid in Hastings*, advertised his plane but he didn't know how to fly it. He looked around and found Harold Rudd. Harold said he didn't know whether he could fly it or not, but he would come and test it and see if it would fly. They had a crowd watching the maiden flight. He checked the controls and the engine with the knowledge he had gained in a year or two of flying. Then he said he would take it down and taxi it around the runway a couple times. He did this a couple times and then went back to the starting point and said he thought it would fly and he would try it. He took off and flew around for a while, tried banking and climbing, etc. and then landed it. He said it was the best plane he had ever flown. He said," If someone wants to go up with me I'll show you." One of the other pilots said he didn't think he wanted to, but a farmer boy said he would like to go and did. They went up and flew around for about ten minutes, and suddenly the plane headed straight down for the ground. The plane was demolished and Harold was killed. The other guy was badly crippled for life. That was the end of the *Maid in Hastings*.

Airplanes remained rare until World War II was close, and then we began to see frequent military planes. There were several training bases in the area, especially the big one at Grand Island. Dick was fascinated with anything to do with airplanes. Dad smoked Wings cigarettes and at that time each pack had a card in it with a picture of an airplane and a brief description on the back. Dick collected all 150 of them and could identify most of them as they flew over. Both a B-24 and a B-17 made crash landings within ten miles or so of Red Cloud during the war, so we got to see those two up close. Dick's first plane ride was in an old Jenny that came through Red Cloud barnstorming. He did not have enough money but it was apparent that he really wanted to do this and some of his richer siblings contributed enough for his flight.

Economic conditions did not improve much until about the start of World War II. At that time it started raining again, there was more demand for crops, and many people began to get jobs in defense plants. There was a large bomb-loading plant near Hastings where the explosives were loaded into the bomb and shell casings. Quite a few people from Red Cloud worked there. It is interesting that the blond people's hair turned green after they worked there long enough, and their skin turned a little yellow. It makes you suspect that environmental controls were not quite as strict as they might have been. While Dick was in high school there was a major explosion in the plant, which was clearly felt in the assembly hall nearly fifty miles away. Some of the kids who had parents working there started crying. There were some deaths from Red Cloud, as we recall.

# 10

# *Veterinary Medicine on the Farm*

This chapter concerns some of the veterinary problems that we experienced on our farm. We administered most of the veterinary care to our animals ourselves. There was a veterinary in Red Cloud named Doc Hurst, but for some reason or other we never used his services. There was a Dr. Moranville in Guide Rock, who was said to be pretty good, but most of our work was done by a self-taught man named Con Wilson. When something really severe or unusual came along, there was a friend of Alf's named Dr. Asher, who we think came from Hastings. One time Alf had a cryptorchid horse that he tried to work as a stud but found his disposition was not amenable to farm work. Doc Asher came down and we restrained the horse, and with no further anaesthesia Doc Asher was ready to dissect his way up into the inguinal canal and find the testis. Allan remembers him extending his arm fully into the scrotum.

Diseases of the horses were fairly few. One year there was an epidemic of sleeping sickness or equine encephalitis, which killed many horses in the area. There was an organization in Hastings that gathered up carcasses for rendering. They were working night and day during those weeks. We didn't lose any animals and we always thought it was because we had mostly mules, which were thought to be immune to the encephalitis. Whether that was true or not we do not know. In earlier times, there was an epidemic of disease that killed horses around 1917. Mal's father-in-law had a considerable herd of fine horses and lost all but two of them. One of the side stories of about that time revolved around a new young doctor, Dr. Creighton, who had just come to town. He thought that he knew the cause of this disease, and claimed that it was the same disease that caused blackleg in cattle. His answer to the problem was to vaccinate all of the horses with the same antigen used for blackleg. Apparently, the results were far from successful and it was said that he was advised to leave town for a while because of the attitude of all of the people who had lost horses.

As far as the blackleg of cattle was concerned, that was a clostridial disease much like gas gangrene in humans. It was uniformly fatal and quite contagious. We always routinely immunized our calves and any young animals that we bought. Apparently, small animals were attacked more than mature animals. The vaccine was apparently made from diseased, crushed material from infected cattle and we injected it into the neck. We always injected mature cattle in the trucks and trailers when they brought the animals in, and the calves when we brought them in in the fall. Bloat was a fairly frequent problem in cattle and was caused by eating of sorghum-type of forage. It was more common in the fall when plants were more mature. Allan thinks it was caused by hydrocyanic acid from the forage material. The animals would bloat until they had difficulty with digestion and sometimes respiration. The treatment was to stab one of the stomachs, probably the rumen, and it was done just back of the last rib. Our father always did this. When Allan started to college, he learned that there was a trocar made for this purpose and suggested it to him. He sort of pooh-poohed the idea and felt that a jack knife was perfectly fine. It seemed that all of the animals that he had treated survived. Brucellosis was fairly common in cattle at that time and the main problem it caused was abortion. The bacillus was Brucella abortis Bang, so we called it Bang's disease. There were skin tests available for this disease and on at least one occasion, the government sent people around to do skin tests on reproducing animals. We do not remember of any of ours testing positive; however, it was a fact that any animals that aborted were fattened and sold for butchering. The government testing was also tried on occasion for tuberculosis. Sometimes government representatives came in and did tuberculin tests on our milk cows. We do not remember ever having any test positive.

Cholera was an ever-present problem with hogs. After Alf had started his farming on a private basis, he had gone into the hog business quite extensively and had a number of litters of small pigs that were attacked by cholera, and he lost 50% of his animals. In later years, we always immunized our animals against cholera. Any new litters or any newly purchased pigs were immunized. Immunization was given in two shots. One was an antigen prepared from infected material, and the other was an antibody to prevent undue destructive material. Most of the time, Con Wilson came and administered the vaccine but later during World War II when labor was scarce, we were able to get the vaccine and do it ourselves. In retrospect this was probably illegal but it was common practice at that time. Not only did we do it ourselves, but Alf, especially, was called upon to help neighbors with immunizations and castrations. Usually, immunization and castration were done on animals at the same time.

Surgery on animals was fairly rare and quite crude. Dehorning was routine for our feeding cattle. Earlier we had Herefords, which were horned, and inasmuch as horned cattle did considerable damage to one another as far as their hides and meat were concerned, we always dehorned them. Dehorning was unpleasant because there was quite a bit of bleeding. By the time we had done a number of cattle, the walls of the corral were sprayed with blood and often we were too. Complications of dehorning were fairly few. Sometimes there was excessive bleeding but not enough to require any special treatment. Occasionally, insects would infect the wound and cause maggots to appear. This may have been a disease with the maggots invading the tissues or it may have been that they were just scavenging dead tissue—probably the latter. Our treatment for that was to pour turpentine into the horn wound. Later on as the war developed, Herefords became less desirable because they required more labor, especially in dehorning, and also because their calving was often more difficult. It was at this time that we switched over to Angus, which we did by buying purebred Angus bulls and putting them in with our scrub cattle. Offspring of a prize bull and a scrub cow would be quite high-class beef.

There was a case of a hernia in a young pig that was quite good-sized. Our father repaired it. The pig was held by the feet with the hind end up and the pig was castrated. Then the inguinal ring was sutured with flour sack string. The pig survived OK. There was one instance of a very small cow delivering a large calf in a breech position. She labored for a couple days and finally Doc Asher came and dismembered the calf but the cow died.

There were several instances of cases of lumpy jaw in cattle. This was actinomycosis, a mold, and was treated by incision and drainage, which was done by Dad with his pocketknife and with apparent total cures. The disease does affect man but we never heard of a case in that area. There were several cases of so-called milk fever that occurred. They occurred in cows that were heavy milkers and delivered a calf without any intervening time in their lactation. This was not really a fever but a deprivation of calcium, losing so much to the milk with the final insult of calving. These cows would go down and be unable to arise. A veterinarian would arrive, probably Con Wilson, and treat them with an intravenous injection of calcium into a neck vein. The result was miraculous, with the cow immediately getting up and foraging. Many years later this was the subject of an episode of the PBS TV program, *"All Things Large and Small"*. It was planned that the next breeding would be delayed, giving the cow a chance to catch up on her calcium stores. Dad kept a record of all the breeding times of the milk cows, which was penciled on the wall of the scale house. Nobody else ever understood his system but it seemed that he always knew which cow was going to calve and when.

A frequent problem was mastitis in milk cows. This was manifested by increasing firmness in the udder of the cow and delivery of clot-like masses in the milk. It usually came in high producers soon after calving and usually cleared by itself. It is to be remembered that none of the milk was pasteurized at that time, and the cows having this problem had God knows what bacteria in their milk that was not separated. In severe cases of mastitis there was a treatment where a needle-like cannula was inserted through the teat into the udder and air was injected. It was said that the pressure of the air stopped the production of milk and allowed the udder time to heal. This should probably be referred to the raised-eyebrow department.

The Rudd family were neighbors of ours. The wife was kind of a hard-boiled woman and did a lot of the farm work—more like a man than a woman. Her name was Edith and everyone called her Old Eed. One year she raised a whole bunch of chickens. Farmers at that time put their potato crop in a cellar or sometimes in an open pit covered with straw and dirt so that they wouldn't freeze in the wintertime, and they would keep until spring. She got the potatoes out of the pit or cellar and they had a lot of sprouts on them about a half-inch long. She went through several bushels of them and took off the sprouts. She scattered them out in the yard and thought maybe that the chickens would eat them. The chickens loved them and ate them all as fast as they could. The next day she found that some of the chickens were lying dead. She looked at some of them and found that their crops were very distended and they had not been able to digest the potato sprouts. She thought they were all going to die so she took some that were still walking around, got a knife, and opened them up and cleaned out their crops. She stitched them up with a needle and thread and they walked away. She did that with all that were left and the story is that she saved 90% of them.

Con Wilson had been called once to clean a cow that had failed to deliver the calf bed. By the time he arrived, this was a very foul smelling, messy job. Dick and Dad were observing and providing some help. Neither of them had the strongest of stomachs and both were wishing they were somewhere else. In the middle of the job, Con withdrew the arm he had had inside the cow, reached into his shirt pocket with that hand, and pulled out a plug of chewing tobacco that he offered to Dad. Dad turned slightly green and left the barn. Dick was amused enough at Dad's discomfort that he managed to stay to the end.

During WWII, the shortage of veterinarians was even more acute. Often we were not able to get one at all in time to do any good. Dick was the only one home and the caliber of the hired men we could get was extremely low. We were often forced to do the best we could on our own and sometimes it was pretty primitive. At one time, we had a cow that could not deliver her calf. Our best efforts to help were ineffective and we could not get anyone to come. Finally, in desperation, we tied the cow to a post and the calf to a team of mules and removed the calf. Surprisingly, the cow survived. On another occasion we used fence-wire stretchers to remove a calf. In that case both the cow and calf survived.

We usually had lots of cats—at least 20 at one time. These were not so much pets as working animals to catch rodents. They got a pan of skim milk once a day but beyond that were expected to fend for themselves. Dad did not like dogs but occasionally one of us would have a dog. The last dog we had was a mostly German Shepherd stray that Dick wanted to keep and Dad did not. Before this was resolved, Mom was home alone one day and saw a tramp coming up the sidewalk. He was a rough-looking man and she was a little frightened. The dog met him half way up the sidewalk and would not let him come any further so the tramp turned and left. After that Mom was on the dog's side and Dad had no chance of getting rid of him. It was never even considered that one would spend money for veterinary care for these dogs and cats. If they got sick, they lived or died on their own. Wounds were treated with axle grease to keep the flies out of the wound.

# 11

# *The 1935 Republican River Flood*

I n June of 1935, we had lots of rain and the Republican River flooded from a broken dam 50 miles west of us. It did a great deal of damage and took several lives. We had had reports of this flood coming down from the west and these reports were sort of pooh-poohed by our father. The river had flooded frequently over the years but those floods were the result of heavy rains up river, which made the river overflow its banks rather slowly. In this great flood, two large tributaries, Frenchman and Prairie Dog Creeks, had become so engorged that a large earth dam burst and a wall of water came down the valley. Our mother became very agitated over these reports and wanted to make plans to evacuate at least some of our farm machinery on the river-bottom land but our father vetoed all of this. As Mom became more and more worried about all this he at one point said "Let's all get in the car and go up to our Uncle Laurence's and watch the river rise." We had a minister of some sort named Wes Price who was working for us at that time. He was courting Polly and through that recommendation came to work for us for a very short time. We all got in the car, including Wes, and started west along the river road. Our mother continued to express great concern that we should be on this low-lying road. At one point, Dad said jokingly, "Wesley, look out the window and see if you can see it coming." Wesley leaned out the window and said, "My God, it is." We were able to turn around and get back to higher ground safely.

Alf and a neighbor, Earl Wilmot, had built a flat-bottomed boat about 10 or 12 feet long of angle iron and sheet metal, with a Model T Ford engine. They took it to a small lake to try it and it did fine. In the river it did well going down stream but could only do about four or five miles per hour upstream. The sheriff of Franklin County, the next county west of ours, had issued a call for boats to rescue people from trees and houses who were in danger of drowning. There were very few boats in the area in those days so Alf and Earl responded, loaded their boat and rushed up to the Naponee and Republican City area. Alf and another man launched the boat about a mile upstream from where people were stranded up to a mile from shore. The river was raging and there was much trash in the water, including some big trees. They had to go downstream backwards because in many places the current was too fast for them to go upstream. They tried to get close enough to trees and houses to get people to jump into the water and then pull them into the boat. Water was coming into the boat and they had to bail frantically to keep it afloat. They made it to shore, only to be told that there were more people in trees at another place. They repeated this process all day and saved several lives. At one point their spark plugs became so fouled that the engine was not working. The sheriff simply went to a line of spectators' cars and confiscated a new set of plugs. Alf was so near death several times that day and saw some die that he was trying to save, that he suffered from nightmares for several weeks afterwards. It was a couple weeks before he could get home again.

The flood took out our telephone lines and our power lines for the rest of the summer. We were able to adapt to the situation by using kerosene lamps, and we had a washing machine that was run by hand cranking. Both the Inavale and Red Cloud bridges were washed out, and in order to get to the other side of the river, we had to go to Riverton to find the only surviving bridge in the area. For some time we had to go south into Kansas to do any shopping. After a few weeks, the merchants in Red Cloud hired two small boats to ferry people across the river near where the bridge had been. On the other side they had trucks to bring the farmers on in to town. At the place where the Inavale bridge had been, for some time there was a temporary suspension bridge. It was just wide enough for a car and swayed and rattled alarmingly when you drove across it. We had to reconstruct our own power line, which crossed the river at the Inavale bridge and ran up to the highway at Inavale. Our father, two of his siblings and one other neighbor had built their own power line years before. (The Rural Electrification Administration did not electrify most of that area until after WWII). After the devastation was cleared, we ran the telephone line across the river again. It was Allan's lot to carry the line across the river. During the passage across the river, someone cranked a phone somewhere and gave him a tremendous shock, which he remembers to this day.

The water rose up to cover the fence just below a small rise to what we called the second bottom land, perhaps a hundred yards from the house. There was a huge amount of debris of all kinds in the water. At one point a chicken coop floated by, covered with squawking chickens. The men salvaged quite a bit of useful lumber from the flood with ropes and we used it for years afterwards. The flood left an enormous amount of debris scattered over the fields that had been flooded—trees, massed barbed wire, wrecked buildings and dead animals. Some areas of prime river bottom land were covered with several feet of sand. We did not have this problem but our bottom land was infested with cockleburs for several years, until we finally got rid of them. Although we had none in our area, there were a number of deaths recorded. Several of these were not found for some time. There were a number of places up and down the river where the floodwaters scooped out holes down below the water level and they filled up and remained for many years as ponds. Although they ruined some farmland, they became useful for recreation, swimming and fishing. At least one of these ponds still exists south of Red Cloud. Our only losses were several stacks of alfalfa hay, a Jayhawk hay stacker, and one of our two hay sweeps. Both of them were swept away and the wooden sweep was never found, but the metal one was found and was repairable.

Allan remembers on one occasion helping to put up ice from one of these ponds. This was the last time he remembers helping put up ice, just about at the start of WWII. It had been an uncommonly cold period, during which a thick layer of ice formed on this pond. The ground was frozen so hard and so icy that horses and mules could not get traction to pull wagons to haul the ice. Allan used an old Case tractor with lugs. It was far below zero weather and the oil in the crankcase was so solid that the engine could not be started. We built a fire under the crankcase and were finally able to turn it over and get it started. Then we had to take a blowtorch to the transmission case so that we could get it warmed up enough to shift gears. We also had to take the blowtorch to the connecting joints on the steering mechanism. After we started cutting the ice, it was so cold that if water splashed on you, it froze before it hit your clothes and you never got wet.

Only a few days after the flood, Mal left the farm because of several consecutive years of drought, dust bowl and no crops. He, with Wes Price and another man, left for California, leaving his best girl behind. She said she thought she would never see him again because she thought all of the girls in California were beautiful movie stars. Mal did stay in California for a year and then went back and farmed some of Dad's land for three or four months. There was another drought and complete crop failure but he married that same girl. They then went to California to make their home for many years.

# 12

## *Farm Work*

L ooking back at farming in general, you can see that most of the procedures were primitive by today's standards. Such things as soil conservation and the use of fertilizer on the soil were just as poorly developed as treatment of some of the animal diseases. With the onset of the dust bowl and the depression, farming became a much harder way to make a living. Dad was a pioneer in early advances in soil conservation. Building of earth dams was something that was unheard of prior to that time. He was instrumental in building four dams to prevent erosion from rainfall and for storage of water for cattle use. This was done in a very laborious way in those days with a Fresno scraper and four horses or mules. This was extremely long, hard and arduous work. Later on after WWII, Polly's husband, Bill Koon, went into business with an earth-moving outfit, which made the work much easier and more efficient. As Alf developed in his farming career, he became much more advanced and much more progressive in his farming technique. Rotation of crops became a serious matter, with the growing of legume crops between years of field crops and grains to maintain nitrogen levels. Alfalfa was an especially good crop for this area and this time. Alfalfa had the ability to drop roots ten or fifteen feet or more and tap ground water not available to field crops. Paradoxically, as times became drier, the alfalfa crop became more profitable. Since it would not grow tall enough for hay it was allowed to seed. Alfalfa seed was a very lucrative business. It was very difficult to harvest. It had to be handled gently in order not to shell out the seeds. It had to be put in windrows in order to dry further and then brought by hand to a separator. Allan remembers tending the separator for this and it was a chore to get it to separate out the seeds and give a clean product. Rain at any stage of this project was a disaster. After it came from the separator, it still had to be cleaned with a small cleaning machine that used air and screens. At one point at least, the cleaned seed sold for $1 per pound. We sometimes planted the rejected chaff for our own purposes. There was enough seed left in it to work if you planted it heavily. Alf became involved with the county agricultural people in an attempt to learn new techniques in soil conservation. He was a pioneer in terracing hillside fields to prevent erosion. Bill Koon also became involved in this at a later time. One of the big things Alf did eventually was to abandon farming on some of the bad lands that were so unproductive for so many years. Some of this land should never have been broken from prairie in the first place and was probably broken as a result of WWI. Wheat was scarce and prices were high but as the soil fertility declined without the addition of water and nutrients, the yields declined to the point that it was no longer profitable. It was Alf who engineered the switch from the Hereford breed of beef cattle to the Angus. It was also Alf who introduced the idea of having tractor power. Our first tractor came in the mid 1930's. It was probably one of the biggest things on the farm to help alleviate difficult labor and aggravation. Looking back, it is hard to imagine hooking up four to six horses or mules abreast and turning in a day's work. It required an enormous amount of skill and stamina.

When successive years of crop failure occurred, atlas sorgo was introduced to make ensilage, which we stored in long trench silos dug out with the old Fresno scraper. Failed corn crops were also used for this purpose. This took the place of the old corn binder, to some extent, rendering the stunted crops more nutritious and more available than the dry fodder had been previously. There was also a certain amount of heat of fermentation generated. In the winter, we backed a wagon into these trench silos and loaded up ensilage to feed the animals. It was warm down there and out of the wind. The aroma was nice and it made kind of a pleasant interlude from the foul weather that was often up above.

Possibly the most boring work was plowing or cultivating with a tractor. One went back and forth, back and forth, with just a slight break when you turned around at the edges of the field, which might be one-quarter to one-half mile apart. In the spring when plowing or corn planting was going on, flocks of seagulls always appeared to feast on the exposed worms. They would circle very low over the tractor. One day, a very bored Alf impulsively reached up and grabbed one by the legs. The seagull emptied his body from every orifice all over him. Alf had to stop work and go home for a bath and complete change of clothes before he could stand to continue.

In regard to farm chores, one of the most distasteful jobs was fixing fence. Digging post holes by hand and stringing recalcitrant barbed wire was not only unpleasant but dangerous. We should have had protective clothing to do this work. It was a job that was often done at times when freezing or rain kept us out of the fields. After heavy rains, fences would sometimes wash out and would have to be replaced and this was a particularly offensive job. We often used osage orange "hedge" posts, and driving a staple in them was like driving them into a steel beam. It was conducive to very unchristian thinking and speech.

There were other rainy-day jobs that came along to keep us all busy. One that was not too bad was cleaning out barns and chicken coops. Although a little aromatic, it was usually warm and dry and out of the wind. Another rainy-day job was fixing harness, which was a never-ending job. There was always harness that had broken and worn out. Grinding sickles for the mowers was also a rainy-day job and this was always a kind of pleasant thing to do. It was done with an old foot-driven grinding wheel made of some sort of sandstone-like material. A segment of automobile tire under the wheel kept it wet. After the wheel soaked for a time in the water, it would develop a soft spot that eventually wore into a notch. That was one of the better rainy-day jobs, since it could be done inside with no mud where everything was warm and dry.

For several years, Allan attended Alf's separator as they moved from farm to farm, threshing mainly field crops. His job at that time consisted of keeping things running, greasing and oiling bearings and keeping them from burning out, repairing belts and moving machinery from farm to farm between jobs. It was hard, dirty work, but it was really quite a lot of fun because most of the farmers were happy in that they had some crops for a change. The food was tremendous. During threshing, the neighbors would all pitch in and the women would all try to outdo themselves and the noon meals were fantastic: three or four entrees, roast beef, chicken and ham and several kinds of dessert, homemade pies and all the trimmings. On several occasions, if they were working in a remote area, the women would bring out the noon meal in the field with the dishes served on bales of hay. There was never more gourmet eating. With the advent of WWII and the combine, this method of harvesting became obsolete. At the farm sale years later, the cherished old Case separator that Allan had tended so dearly was sold for $5 for junk. It was the end of an era.

The big furnace in the house consumed huge amounts of firewood. Usually, dead or sick trees, mostly cottonwood, were cut down during summer rainy spells when the fields were too wet to work. The trees were just left lying where they fell to dry over the summer. In the winter, we sawed them into about five-or six-foot lengths and split the larger logs with wedges and a maul. The colder it was the better the cottonwood split. This was before the days of chainsaws, and it was all sawed with a two-man crosscut saw. This was hard work and you could be stripped to your shirt and sweating while the bottom half of you was so cold it was numb. The wood was hauled in wagons and slid through a basement window near the furnace. We had a buzz saw made from a Model T Ford for cutting the smaller branches into wood for the cookstove.

Dad did most of the milking with the aid of whoever was available except Polly. This was not a fun job. In the summer, the flies were thick and fierce. One cow, particularly, would monotonously whack you on the back of your head with her tail without ever missing. In the winter it was a cold job. A Holstein cow that we milked had very small teats so that your lower fingers inevitably got wet and then colder than ever. That cow always stood very well, but, infrequently, would lift her leg and quite deliberately stick it in the bucket of milk and then kick it and you across the barn. Every cow had a name and a personality of her own, unlike the feedlot cattle.

In those days, corn was husked by hand. You wore a leather palm which had a steel hook attached to it. You tore the hook across the husks exposing the ear of corn, grabbed the ear with the other hand, twisted it off and threw it into a wagon moving alongside. The wagon had a bang board mounted on the far side. This work looked deceptively easy if you watched an expert. A good cornhusker could pick over 100 bushels a day and would have one ear of corn in the air all the time. Dick and a town friend, Jerry Anderson, sometimes husked corn for Dad on Sunday to make a little spending money. If they worked hard the two of them might get 30 or 40 bushels. The pay was ten cents a bushel and food and lodging. Success depended partly on having a good team to pull the wagon. A good team would keep moving up whenever they sensed you getting toward the front of the wagon, while a bad team required a lot of loud instruction.

Lucille, Alf's wife, was an uncut diamond. Lucille was a good cook and made the best barbecued spareribs ever eaten. She was always more interested in the outdoor work than in housework or traditional feminine activities. After the girls got bigger and did not need constant attention, she had a little Ford tractor and liked working that more than anything. She also had many other skills commensurate with those of her husband, both in the home and in the fields. During the summer that Allan came home from Germany and left the army, he did not have a medical license and could not practice, so he and his family stayed in Red Cloud for the birth of their second child. He spent the summer working with Alf and Lucille in the fields. The three of them could turn out as much work as any three men and maybe four.

The farm work was made more unpleasant by the Nebraska weather. It seemed like it was always either too cold, too hot, too wet or too dry. There were frequent thunderstorms and "gully washers" that damaged crops and fences. Hailstorms could wipe out a crop in a few minutes as well as break windows and damage roofs. We were in tornado alley and frequently there were tornadoes in the area. Our farm did not suffer much damage from tornadoes. One cut off a corner of an abandoned barn on what we called the Parkinson place. Another struck near Alf's house during the night. We had been building a new corncrib and just had the framing up. It was badly twisted but we straightened it up and finished the construction. That was probably a mistake since it was never really square in any direction. We saw that a hayrack had been picked off its running gear and deposited in a field about one hundred yards away. It was not until several days later that we realized all that had really happened. The wind had removed that hayrack and then picked up a second hayrack that it dropped neatly on the running gear that the first hayrack had been on. It dropped it with no damage and so perfectly aligned that we would not have noticed it if it had not put it on backwards!

# 13

## *Fun and Games*

Although all of us kids did work on the farm according to our size and ability, there was plenty of time for fun. There was not a lot of money available for toys, especially during the depression and drought years. We made many of the things we played with ourselves from materials that were available free. These were materials such as rubber bands cut from inner tubes, wooden orange crates, wooden cigar boxes, and old wagon and buggy wheels. Unfortunately, most of these materials are no longer available or have become valuable antiques. When we tried to show our children how to make some of our toys, we could not do it with the materials that we had used. When we had to go out and buy substitute materials, part of the point of the exercise was lost. It is a pity since we had as much fun making the toys as playing with them, and we learned useful skills in the process.

All of us made and flew kites. These were usually simple flat kites made from orange crates and covered with newspaper. Newspaper was the biggest sheet of paper we had available and limited the size of the kite. To glue the newspaper to the frame we used paste made from flour and water. We had a homemade crank-driven string winder and over a mile of string. The wind on the prairie was almost always kind to kite flyers. Newspaper was not the ideal material and most kites ended their lives when the paper tore. In one case, a half-dozen Arkansas kingbirds returning from driving away a hawk encountered our kite and literally pecked it to pieces before we could retrieve it. Dick wanted to make his own kite by himself before he was old enough to handle the sticks and strings, so he cut one out of a large cardboard box. To everyone's surprise, it actually flew.

Many of our toys we either threw or flew. Most of them would probably now be considered too dangerous for children to play with. The teeth on mower bars had to be replaced when they became too worn. These discarded teeth were great toys to throw at buildings where they would embed themselves a half-inch or more and stick. We were allowed to throw these and the darts described below only at the cob house and an abandoned shed since they did considerable damage. We would chalk up targets and play games similar to darts with these. We made darts out of broken pitchfork or broom handles. A piece four or five inches long was cut and a nail driven coaxially into one end with about an inch sticking out. We then cut off the nail head and filed the nail to a sharp point. On the other end we made two holes by driving and removing nails so that we could stick two chicken wing feathers in for stabilization. The result was quite a good dart that could be driven all the way into the side of a building. In retrospect, it is surprising that Dad let us use the side of the cob house since it was quite hard on the building.

Another, less lethal, dart was whittled out of an old shingle. The thick end of the shingle was whittled down to a narrow strip, maybe 3/4 of an inch wide with a point at the end. At the thin end of the shingle, it widened out to two or three inches. A notch was cut near the point so that we could attach a sling, which was a stick with either a piece of cord or a rubber band tied on it. You could throw these practically out of sight with a little practice. They were surprisingly stable, considering that they only had a vane in one plane.

Most of the above toys required a pocketknife, or jack knife as we called it. Every farmer carried one and almost every boy did as well. They were useful tools and they were toys in themselves. We used to play mumblety-peg or root-the-peg, which involved flipping the knife in various ways and making it stick in the ground. Some of these ways were a little hazardous since they involved standing the knife on its point on some part of your body and flipping it with your finger. The penalty for losing this game was to have to draw out a peg driven into the ground with your teeth. Two different forms of this game were played and we do not recall the exact differences between them. Older boys sometimes played a game where they took turns flipping the knife into the ground, trying to damage or break the opponent's knife. The knives were kept very sharp in order to be useful and were carried everywhere. Now boys are sent home from school or suspended for carrying the smallest knife to school. Are kids now more vicious or are we just more safety conscious?

The natural rubber inner tubes of the day made great rubber bands and you could cut them as wide as you wanted. With these we made "rubber guns". Usually these were crude pistol-shaped pieces of one-inch wood with a spring clothespin nailed to the back of the grip. A rubber band was stretched over the muzzle end and the doubled end was pinched in the clothespin. When you squeezed the grip it fired the rubber band. At one time we made a "machine gun". This was a rifle-shaped piece of wood with notches cut along the top of the "barrel". Rubber bands were stretched from the muzzle and hooked over each of these notches. A piece of fish line was fastened near the muzzle and went under each of these notches and then to a crank mounted on the stock. As you turned the crank, the string tightened and lifted each rubber band off its notch in turn. Groups of boys would get together for rubber gun fights on Saturdays on occasion.

We made slingshots out of forked tree branches and the same rubber bands. The power of these was limited only by the strength available to pull them. We could kill sparrows with them if we could hit them. Dick hit a mourning dove with his, using just a small, hard clod of dirt. The dove came tumbling down and Dick was holding it in his hand feeling very badly when it suddenly revived and flew away. Mostly we used them to shoot at cans and targets.

We used to try to make bows and arrows but we never had anything but green wood to work with and they were never very successful.

Since none of us had ever seen a real bow and arrow, we really did not have much idea what to try to do.

Dick was given a toy helicopter, which consisted of an aluminum propeller with a circle of wire attached to the tips of the propeller. It was launched with a spool sitting on top of a stick. Two little pins on top of the spool engaged two holes in the center of the propeller. You wound a string around the spool and then pulled it to get the propeller rotating. It flew very well and was a great toy but the aluminum propeller did not last very long. Dick found he could cut propellers out of the bottoms of tin cans that flew well without the wire circle around them. These were a little more dangerous, since the sharp and somewhat raggedly cut propeller tips could hit you, but a little cut now and then did not bother him. Eventually, Dick decided that he wanted something bigger and better. He cut a propeller out of an old windmill fan, which was heavy-gauge galvanized steel and about 24 inches long. He laboriously hammered this into the proper shape. He made a spool out of an old binder roller and mounted it on top of a fence post. He used clothesline rope instead of string. When it was time to flight test it, Dick heaved on the rope as hard as he could. The propeller rose up a few inches off the spool roaring like a lawnmower engine and then swooped down over his head as he ducked. It hit a tree nearby and cut a gash about three inches deep. He never had the courage to try it again.

Another class of toys we made was rolling toys. Many of the farms in those days had the remains of one or more buggies. If you stripped off the body and the tongue or shafts and put a board on the running gear to sit on, you had a fine "coaster". You tied a rope to each end of the front axle near the wheel so you could steer them (sort of). With the big wheels, you could coast in the pasture or any rough ground. Unfortunately, there always seemed to be a barbed wire fence at the foot of each good hill. The idea was to turn parallel to the fence before you hit it, but with the crude steering and no brakes, we would more often than not have to bail out when we saw that we were going to hit the fence. We had lots of bruises, cuts and scrapes but never any serious injuries.

There were also steel rims from old wooden wagon wheels around. With an appropriate size, you could brace yourself inside one of these rims and with someone else's help you could start rolling down a hill, head over heels. These rides also invariably wound up in a crash and extreme dizziness.

Polly remembers "scooters" made with roller skate wheels and a wooden box. There was a sidewalk going to the outdoor privy, which was somewhat downhill. She remembers a memorable crash she had into the privy.

We made and walked on stilts quite a bit. Often we would take these to school, actually walking on them one mile to school, and play running games on them. These were usually made out of one by four boards with a piece of two by four nailed on for a footrest. Often the footrest was supported by an old piece of harness leather. The top of the stilt was cut down to handgrip size with a drawknife, our only woodworking tool. They were not really very good stilts since they were heavy and the one by four tended to split and break with use, but we had a lot of fun with them.

We used to play a game called "shinny". This was vaguely like hockey on land. We used a stick cut from the branch of a tree, leaving about six inches of the thicker branch for the head and the thinner branch cut to an appropriate length for the handle. A tin can was used instead of a puck. It was a rough game. If the tin can hit you, it hurt, and if your opponent got off side, you were allowed to hit him on the shins with your stick. We suppose that is the origin of the name.

We made a lot of wooden swords from stakes from an abandoned snow fence. Shields were cut from cardboard boxes and sunflower stalks in the fall were used for spears and lances. The drawknife was used to sharpen the swords.

The drawknife was a very useful tool and was used in making many of our toys. Dick wanted a baseball bat of his own and made one out of a broken wagon tongue, shaping it with the drawknife. It was too short but made up for it by being too thick, and overall was quite satisfactory.

In the summer, we spent a lot of time swimming or at least in the water. The Republican River was not dammed then but it was often difficult to find a place that was deep enough to swim. There were some farm ponds that we swam in that were probably too contaminated for safety. In the Nebraska summer heat, we were not too picky about water quality as long as it cooled us off. After the 1935 flood, there were some ponds washed out on the river bottomland that were pretty good for swimming. These were apparently connected to the river through a layer of sand and rose and fell with the river level. This kept them flushed enough to keep from getting stagnant. They also provided some pretty good fishing with lots of bullheads and big-mouth bass.

We also dug caves in the summer. These were dug on flat ground, roofed with old boards or branches and then covered with dirt. We made lamps to use in them with a rag wick in a tin-can lid filled with kerosene. These had varied uses as pirate caves, old settler dugouts, etc., and were nice and cool. Unfortunately, they also were attractive to lizards, toads and bugs of many kinds and soon became uninhabitable.

In the winter we did some ice-skating but it was seldom that the water froze smooth. Usually, there was some snow so that the surface was half-frozen snow and no good for skating. We had several pairs of skates of the type that clamped onto your shoes and came off much easier than they went on. There was also sledding using real sleds, corn scoop shovels and a large galvanized dish pan of Mom's.

We played cards a lot. We played pitch, high fives, cribbage, several varieties of rummy, pinochle and poker for matches. When we visited our Aunt Soph and Uncle Trace, we played whist. Most of us learned or honed our skills at addition playing cribbage. Monopoly was popular. We played horseshoes using old mule shoes. We also read a lot. We had a small collection of books, which were read and reread. Whenever we went to Red Cloud, there was a visit to the library. You could only check out one book per card but with the five of us and Mom and Dad having cards, there were usually enough cards in the library to get several new books.

Radio was fairly popular. We had a big console radio that did not get very good reception. We never used it to listen to music but there were some programs that we liked to listen to. We liked Jack Benny, Fred Allen, Amos and Andy, Fibber McGee and Molly, and Charlie McCarthy. We also listened to Major Bowes' *Original Amateur Hour* and we kids sometimes listened to the *Lone Ranger, Jack Armstrong the All-American Boy*, and other such programs. We liked *Suspense* and the *Inner Sanctum* and *The Shadow,* but Mom was always afraid that they would give us nightmares. Mom listened to some soaps—the only one that comes to mind is "*The Romance of Helen Trent*".

Girls in those days played much the same games as they do now, with heavy involvement with dolls. Polly did all of these girl things but she also tagged along behind her two older brothers, doing or attempting to do everything that they did. With Mom's illness, she was pushed into more housework and cooking at an earlier age than she would have preferred.

All in all, there were lots of fun things for kids to do. In later years, as more of the smaller farms were merged, there was a problem of other kids to play with but usually there were at least one or two within a two-mile pony ride. In Dick's time, our rural mail carrier, "Goob" Leonard, organized a baseball team for the boys. They practiced or played a game once a week in Inavale, which meant a four-mile pony ride each way for Dick. Between the little village and the surrounding farms, there were enough boys to make a team. Dick remembers that only the catcher and the first baseman had gloves, which belonged to Goob. Nobody on the team had his own glove. When Goob could find opponents in nearby towns, they would all load into a cattle truck and go off to play. Goob also took them off on swimming trips a couple times—once to a real swimming pool.

# 14

## *Food*

We have noted that we raised much of our own food. Fresh meat waited for the advent of the cold season, as we had no means of refrigeration. On the day of the first butchering with the approach of winter, there was always a special pig that had been prepared suitably and it was quite an exciting day. The pig was killed by severing its carotic and allowing it to bleed to death. The pig was scalded in a large iron kettle and the bristles were removed by scraping it with knives. In later years after Polly married Bill Koon, who was a butcher at the time, he showed us how to skin the pig. This was much less laborious than scalding and scraping off the bristles. The pig was hoisted in a tree by its hind legs and a singletree and gutted and allowed to cool. The supper that night consisted of the most perishable part, the liver, which was prepared in a family recipe, called Poor Man's Dish." This was a liver, potato and onion dish with a succulent gravy and covered with biscuits. To this day, we still relish liver and onions and Poor Man's Dish, and it always reminds us of that first night after having gone through the summer without much fresh meat. When Dick was in college, he worked with a girl who claimed she liked every kind of food except liver. Dick said he could make liver so that she would like it and cooked Poor Man's Dish. She said that she still didn't really like it but it was better than any other liver she had ever had. About the time Dick finished his Ph.D., she married a man in the diplomatic service and went to England. She claimed that she introduced the dish to diplomatic circles as "Dr. McCall's Liver Stew." The truth of this story is unknown. Fried liver with a light gravy was excellent with pancakes in the morning.

The big iron pot on short legs that we used for scalding the pig sat outside in the area where we butchered for many years. It was also used for making soap. Dad saved all of the excess fat trimmed off the carcasses and cooked them in the pot with lye. After the soap cooled into a somewhat soft mass, he cut it up into chunks with a butcher knife. We always used this soap for our laundry. A few days before we had the sale of our farm equipment, someone stole the big iron pot.

As the season progressed, other animals were butchered and the hams and the sides of bacon were saved and cured in the smokehouse. They were smoked with corncobs and green ash wood. Years when one of us was small, someone would save the urinary bladder for them. Inflated with a straw and with the ureters tied off, it made a nice balloon toy. With the spare parts, Dad made a sausage that was one of the best sausages ever. Later in the season, one or more cattle were slaughtered, depending on the number of hired help and the number of family still at home. The cattle were killed with a blow to the head with an axe and then bled out in the same manner as the pigs. Later on, it was realized that this was probably satisfactory kosher technique. Choice chunks of the brisket and bottom round were saved to fill a large stone crock and these were corned. This was done by Dad and we don't know exactly how it was done except that it was a mixture of salt and sodium nitrate and it was adjusted in strength until it would float an egg. That was the end point of the mixture. As we remember, he held it over an open flame in the kerosene stove and seared the outside of the pieces and then put it into the brine and soaked it. The corned beef was primarily saved for summer consumption when the fresh meat was gone. There were also chunks of round that were dried by hanging in the smokehouse to make dried beef. We also canned beef, which had a flavor all its own and still makes us drool every time we think of it. The old system of preparing meat was very complex but at the same time so well integrated that it gave us optimal fresh meat throughout much of the year.

As spring came, we got our brooder chickens from the hatchery and prepared for the summer chicken season. Earlier, we raised some chickens that were hatched under a hen, but later on we obtained chicks from a hatchery in a batch of two or three hundred. Sometime in the mid 1930's we built a second chicken house designed with brooder heating for the small chicks.

At about the time the fresh meat was finished, we would start eating the hams, bacon, and corned beef. By this time, fresh vegetables had been very scarce during the winter, and one of the first fresh vegetable dishes we had was wild lamb's quarters, which were harvested from the fields and roadsides. This went very well with the newly opened hams and bacons. Sunset says that this is Chenopodium Album or pigweed but this is not the weed that we called pigweed. We put vinegar, salt and pepper on it after it was cooked, much like spinach but not as slippery. We liked it much better than spinach. Some people cooked it and added chopped bacon or side meat. During the growing season, we harvested a large part of our vegetables. We always had a potato patch, which we hoped would yield enough potatoes that we could store them through the winter in a pit, covering them with straw and dirt to protect them from the frost. We also had a tomato patch, which gave us enough to eat during the summer with a large amount for canning for winter use. We had a melon patch, which provided enough melons for summer use and once there were so many that we were feeding them to the pigs. Sometimes in the fall, if there was a late frost, we would take some of the melons and cover them with corn shocks to protect them from the frost and thus extend the melon season for some time into the winter. In the outside cellar was a large box of moist sand in which we would bury root crops, mainly carrots and turnips for preservation into the winter months. The cellar was a remarkable storage place. It was immune to freezing, readily accessible and was the site of all of our canned goods storage as well as eggs.

The spring chickens mentioned above were allowed to grow during the summer and the cockerels were butchered as soon as they were big enough to eat. The summer fried chicken was a wonderful invention. A large number of them, were allowed to mature and become hens for laying eggs in the winter. The chickens we raised were Rhode Island Reds. We do not know why Dad always raised them but apparently they were hardy and made large roasting chickens when they matured. One of the bad things about them was that they were very prone to producing pinfeathers and Polly remembers spending considerable time cleaning them. During the winter, we became proficient at culling the hens, separating those that were laying from those that were not. The ones that were not laying became our Sunday roasting chickens or were sold.

One year, several months after we had eaten our last rooster, one of our Rhode Island Red hens showed up with two chicks that she had hatched from a hidden nest. There were no roosters within almost a half-mile and we were puzzled. The chicks grew up, and by the time they were half-grown they could fly beautifully. Rhode Island Reds are so heavy they can hardly fly at all and each night for a while when the chicks flew up into a tree to roost, the poor old hen almost went crazy trying to call them down into the chicken coop. She finally gave up on them and they roosted in the trees until Thanksgiving. At that time Dick, who was the only one still at home, shot them and we had them for Thanksgiving dinner. We always wondered if a rooster pheasant could have been the father.

For several years while Allan was in high school, he did some experiments making some capons. These were nice birds and very good for roasting in the winter, but it was a lot of fuss and bother and never was too successful. Roast chicken with sage dressing and potatoes and gravy was an excellent Sunday dinner.

Most of the families then believed in the Golden Rule and the Ten Commandments and they lived them. Sometimes, there were kids that stole some watermelons but if they did not destroy the rest of the patch, the farmers never cared. When someone went into an orchard and stole some fruit, it was kind of pointless because if you had plenty of fruit, you shared it with neighbors and friends. Sweet corn was something that was often at a premium because you just could not raise it during the dry years except down on the bottom lands. There was little or no irrigation. We always had sweet corn and we usually had watermelons. We did not have an orchard at that time. We were always happy to share what we had. We also made use of what nature furnished. We picked wild grapes, plums, currants and gooseberries and made delicious homemade jelly. Nothing could equal it. It was especially good on homemade bread hot out of the oven.

We took a certain amount of wild game over the seasons. This was usually taken by the younger members of the family and was more of a sport than necessity. There were red squirrels, which were thought to be a delicacy. These were fairly common when we stored the ear corn in piles on the ground. Later on, when we discontinued this practice, they became less common and, at one time, we protected them. Cottontail rabbits were considered good and sometimes jackrabbits were eaten. Eating jackrabbits was frowned upon because they sometimes had a disease that gave them mucinous abdominal tumors. Catfishing was common by the younger set, who would set lines along the river and run them periodically and harvest enough that there would be several messes of catfish during the summer. There were always a bunch of pigeons in the barn, which were considered to be a pest. There were nests along the sides of the barn where they could nest safely. They usually raised two squabs and when they were sufficiently mature we would go up at night and harvest them. If we got enough pigeons, we would have a pigeon pie made in about the same way as a chicken pie with a biscuit crust. Pheasants were quite plentiful and were taken quite often, not always with due regard to the season. Quail, which had been very plentiful in early days, had become an endangered species and Dad would not permit us or anyone else to take quail.

Ducks were taken from the ponds and sometimes from the river. These were not taken very sportingly but shot on the water in order to get the maximum yield per shotgun shell. We liked the bigger ducks and turned up our noses at the teal, which were the most common variety.

On some occasions when the level of water in the river was right, we fashioned a fish trap made of chicken wire and were sometimes able to capture significant numbers of fish at once. This was strictly illegal but game wardens were relatively few in those days. When the Republican River was low and relatively clear, you could wade around in the shallows with a bushel basket and a flashlight and pop the basket down over a catfish, and then reach in through a hole in the bottom and grab it. Once again this was strictly illegal but fishing was mostly for the table rather than sport, and at the time we did not worry too much about those things. On hot days, the catfish tended to lie still in holes in the bank and under logjams, and if you felt around slowly and had quick hands, you could grab them. One day several of the neighbors were doing this and Earl Wilmot said, "Hey, I've got a big carp!" He pulled it out and instead of a carp he had a young beaver by the tail. For a big man standing neck deep in water, he got out of the river amazingly fast. We were mainly interested in the channel catfish but there were other species such as the yellow cat and the mud cat that were considered to be inferior for eating. Two of Dick's friends caught a 50-pound mud cat, which is a very big fish for such a small river. There were also some rather large carp but they were considered to be bony and not very desirable for eating. In later years, someone showed us how to steak the carp, which got rid of most of the bones, and they were then quite good to eat. Sometimes snapping turtles were harvested and they were quite good eating. Our main experience with them was having a string of fish on a line in the river and having a snapping turtle find them and leave only the heads on the string.

We had at least four and sometimes six or seven milk cows at any given time and they were milked night and morning. The milk was separated with a hand-cranked separator and the cream was churned into butter, which was then traded at Burden's grocery store for grocery supplies. They would not pay cash but would give you tokens which were good only at their store. The buttermilk that we got from this process was prized and what we did not consume we were able to sell for 25 cents per gallon, which was a welcome bit of extra cash in those days. It was a very pleasant experience on a hot day to go down to the cool basement when butter was being churned. After the bung was pulled on the churn, one could collect some of the cool buttermilk in a tin can, salt it a little bit and drink it. Buttermilk is still a favorite and frequent food in our family. It was a specially prized food for Bill Koon, who always ordered buttermilk when we went out for dinner if it was available. The skim milk was used by our family to a small degree for drinking. We never did seem to drink whole milk at our house although the skim milk from our separator was probably quite rich. The skim milk that we did not drink was fed to bucket calves or put in buckets and allowed to sour and used for pig and chicken feed. On rare occasions we would make cottage cheese out of it but this was a lot of work and there was not a lot of time in those days for such things. Even more rarely, we made a yellow cheese. The sour-cream butter that we made had a very good flavor and was prized in the community. At Burden's store it was prized not only for the flavor but because our mother, who made the butter, would always round it up over the butter press so there was always an ounce or two extra over a pound.

The cream separator was washed every morning and this was always a chore for the younger members of the family. It was not considered to be an ideal job and it had to be done before school. In spite of the fact that we had no means of pasteurization, we do not remember any illnesses that were attributable to problems with milk products. Our hygienic practices were not always the best.

In spite of our mother's problem with tuberculosis, up to the time of WWII we still te raw ground beef. At the time, we thought it was wonderful on crackers with raw onions, salt and pepper. Probably, we would no longer consider eating it although Dick had some great beef tartar sandwiches in Denmark. One curious aspect of our food was our lack of interest in corn. We had literally tons of corn often lying on the ground and valued only for pig feed, but we never ate much of it ourselves. Once in a while, someone would make some hominy out of it but it was infrequent and not considered to be very good food. We always had sweet corn, which we considered a delicacy during the brief time it was good in the summer. We did dry small amounts of it, which we laid on a screen on the balcony, and protected from insects with nets. It was pretty good but not what you would call a staple. We canned some of it but once again the amounts were small. Several years we raised popcorn and one year we raised a whole wagonload. We ate it for several years and gave a lot of it away but a lot of it wound up being fed to the pigs. In later years we wondered why we didn't take more advantage of the corn as the Mexicans did. About the only cereal food we used was wheat. We did use small amounts of rice but this was used for puddings and dessert. We did not use oats because our father felt that oats were suitable only for animals. Allan doesn't remember having oatmeal until he went in the service. Besides bread, the only major starch source was the potato, which in our family was considered to be a main staple and was often served three times a day.

Another class of food known for its unpopularity was legumes. We did grow beans in the summer. They grew very well, but we used them primarily as green beans. Dick once grew baby lima beans and harvested them as a dry bean. He remembers being disappointed that they were not as good as the Great Northern beans that Mom always bought for dry beans. Nobody else liked them much either. The same was true for peas. We had peas growing very well in the garden and these were used only as a green summer food. It was a wonderful thing when the peas and the new potatoes came along at the same time and we would cook them together in a cream sauce. That was a delicious dish. It must have been that the ready availability of meat at a reasonable price led us to ignore legumes and cereal grains, which were a big part of the diet of many of the world's cultures. This may change radically, beginning at the time of this writing, in days when pollution of subsoil moisture, and water supplies, and diseases such as mad cow disease and foot and mouth disease are beginning to threaten meat supplies. We may turn out to be more vegetarian by necessity than by choice.

Another dish that we liked was pig's knuckles. As the butchering season went along, the pig's feet were saved until there were enough to be significant and then they were cooked in vinegar-flavored solution and allowed to jell. They made a delectable dish. These are available commercially at the grocery store and we still get them once in a while but they are not as good.

We would take junk pieces of meat, such as neck bones, and our mother would boil them and allow them to set into a gelatin-like mass. These were kept out on the back porch in a large crock in the wintertime. It was a wonderful dish to have with pancakes in the morning. The slightly salty gelatin made wonderful syrup for pancakes. Pancakes were a staple for breakfast for the majority of mornings. Usually they were garden-variety pancakes made with buttermilk but in the wintertime we would we would often have sourdough pancakes for a week or two at a time. On rare occasions, we would use the sourdough and make buckwheat pancakes. These made a sour, almost bitter pancake, which was quite good. It was a myth at that time that they were not edible in the summertime because they would cause a rash. We don't know when or how this myth came about but it was generally held to be a fact.

# Epilogue

The authors, who range from 72 to 90 years old, have described just how life was when they were growing up on the farm. We hope that the results are interesting and enjoyable to others, as well as documenting a way of life that is gone forever.

0-595-22760-0